WALKING
BRITTANY COAST

VOL 1:
MONT ST-MICHEL TO MORLAIX

Judy Smith

Walking the Brittany Coast
Vol 1: Mont St-Michel to Morlaix
published by Red Dog Books
ISBN 978 0 9557088 0 0

© text and photos Judy Smith 2008

British Library Cataloguing-in-Publication Data
A catalogue record for this book is available from the British Library

Red Dog Books is based in Axbridge, Somerset and in Brittany.
Enquiries should be addressed to the editorial office at
Red Dog Books, 29410 Plounéour-Ménez, France.

email: reddogbooks@orange.fr

www.reddogbooks.com

Printed and bound in China

For our grandson Nathaniel
We hope that you too will set foot on this splendid coast one day.

About the Author

Judy Smith has been walking in France for over 30 years and is well-known for her informative and entertaining writing. Brittany has long been a favourite destination - *Walking Brittany* was published by Red Dog Books in 2005 - but she has also written walking guides to Normandy, the Loire and Provence, as well as places closer to home in the UK. Her latest works include *Undiscovered France* and the Landmark Visitors' Guide *Vendée and Charente Maritime* as well as *Shropshire Teashop Walks*.

Acknowledgements

Thanks are due to Brittany Ferries for their support and interest in this project, as well as to the very helpful staff of Offices de Tourisme all along this coast.

CONTENTS

ABBREVIATIONS

CA	Continue ahead
L	left
R	right
TJ	T-junction
P	parking
km	kilometre
m	metres

D	Route Départementale (eg D10)
GR	Grand Randonnée (long distance footpath)
Mkt	market
TO	Tourist Office

MAP SYMBOLS

🄰	abbey	⍭	lighthouse
✧	archaeological feature	〰	marsh
✳	belvedere	◊	menhir
⑥	campsite	⬢	mill
①	chambres d'hôte	△	monument
♠	chapel	═	motorway
⁘	château	Ⓜ	museum
♠	church	P	parking
†	cross/calvaire	‖	path limit (see next/previous map)
⊓	dolmen	---	path to follow
◰	electricity station	....	path alternative/detour
≜	fontaine	⤚	picnic area
☆	fort	▦▦▦	railway
②	gîte d'étape	①	rando-plume, rando-gîte
⌂	hamlet	═	road (surfaced)
ⓐ	hotel	●	roundabout
▲	houses	⊕	seamark
▲	houses/town	ƒ	semaphore
▪	lavoir	═	track
		③	youth hostel

6

ABOUT THIS BOOK

This book is intended for anyone and everyone who would like to take a walk along the north coast of Brittany, whether it be just an afternoon's stroll or a whole month's walking holiday that they have in mind. The whole route between Mont St Michel and Morlaix (almost 600km) is fully described with easy-to-follow directions, and is accompanied by practical information on tourist offices, shops, restaurants, accommodation and transport.

The directions given here make for simplicity – they describe a route that hugs the coast as far as it is practically possible, and you should need no more than these to keep you on the right track. Most of the coast is accessible for walking, either by the GR34, a major footpath, other local paths or along beaches (depending on the tides). A certain amount of road walking may be necessary in places, for ease of access or to avoid stretches of littoral impassable because of private property boundaries or unsafe cliffs. Some sections of the route suggested in this book may not be viable at the highest tides and road alternatives are usually suggested.

The introduction gives an overall view of the characteristics of coastal walking and a planning section at the end of the book covers factors to be taken into account when considering a walk along the littoral.

The glossary gives helpful terms of reference and vocabulary.

A list of abbreviations and map symbols used in the text is also included (opposite).

Each main chapter of the book deals with a section of coastline, working west from Mont St-Michel.

A brief introduction gives the overall length and flavour of the route, and highlights its attractions. Directions for walkers are then presented in full, using standard abbreviations (see p.6) in blue text.

The schematic scale maps mark the suggested route by a green broken line. Alternatives and diversions are shown by a dotted line. Each map is numbered and thus linked to the written directions. e.g. 24/3 in the directions refers to point 3 shown on map 24. Map symbols can be found on page 6.

Note on directions The amount of detail in the directions does vary considerably, depending on the complexity of the route: towns and villages often require lengthier explanations than the concise presentation where the route is straightforward. Sometimes the route is obvious and the book is only necessary for back-up at those inevitable points where confusion sets in. Extra detail such as warnings, descriptive phrases and alternative routes are given in bold within the text of directions.

Information about sights along the way or within a short distance of the path is given in black in the text or in separate boxes. This is inevitably selective, and local tourist offices will be able to provide further suggestions for visits in each area.

At the end of each section, a box contains practical information about accommodation, services and transport. This list is not exhaustive, but a starting point for planning walking holidays. Consult the town websites given there for further information. Please note that we cannot guarantee the opening hours/months of shops, bars and restaurants or accommodation.

The places listed under services have at least basic shopping facilities (bakery and/or supermarket, and usually a cash-point) and refreshments in the form of a bar/café. Most have a range of eateries and shops. In the summer season many extra outlets will be open.

Note on Accommodation   A selection of places on or very close to the coastal path is given, with the emphasis on B&B, camping and dormitory accommodation for walkers. This is only a small sample of what is available - the criteria of selection have generally been average prices and all year round opening. In the main, hotels are not listed, unless in special locations, nor B&B in towns – for these, consult the relevant tourist offices (details also given). Much accommodation is seasonal, so the choice will be greatest from June to September.

The transport details are designed primarily to help those planning linear walks, so taxi information and the website of local bus networks are given.

Suggestions for other walks in each area are given in brief. *Walking Brittany*, also by Judy Smith, and *Central Brittany Coast to Coast* by Penny Allen are recommended for further reference.

The planning section at the end of the book has useful advice for preparing to walk the coastal path, with suggestions for the best walking if only a limited time is available.

An index of main place names is also included for ease of reference.

Colour photographs taken by the author are used throughout.

PLEASE READ

It is at all times the responsibility of each individual to decide on the advisability of a walk on the coast with regards to safety in respect of tides, high seas, and strong winds, especially on cliff paths.

Essential equipment should include proper footwear, bad weather protective clothing, an adequate supply of water and some form of communication device, whether a mobile phone or at the very least a whistle. Enjoy coastal walking, but please try to remain safety conscious.

INTRODUCTION

Cliffs, coves and sandy beaches, fishing boats and lighthouses, prehistory, mythology and that vivid azure sea – the best of everything associated with Brittany is here on this magnificent north coast. Brittany is different – a part of France that is not quite French, a Celtic land where fervent religious beliefs go hand-in-hand with deep-seated superstition, an enchanted land of legend and folklore. All Breton life and culture springs from the sea, from the early saints who crossed from Wales or Ireland to evangelise these coasts to the generations of fishermen who have risked their lives for its harvest. The Breton heart beats to the rhythm of the waves, and in walking this path so too will yours.

Five hundred and fifty kilometres of path are described here and obviously only the most fortunate few will have the time to do all that in one go. But this path is so accessible that it can easily be taken in smaller bites – a week, a few days or even an afternoon. As a long-distance walk it benefits from readily available accommodation, while shorter sections can be enjoyed by anyone already holidaying on this coast. And although its nature varies from place to place, nowhere at all is it too demanding. The final bonus is that coming from Britain, this path is simply a ferry ride away. There's no need to take the car, just put on your boots before you descend the gang-plank in St-Malo!

So what are the alluring ingredients of this route? Highlights it has, certainly – Mont St-Michel, France's most visited attraction outside Paris, and the Pink Granite Coast, the most remarkable section of littoral in Brittany – but more importantly there are such contrasts here. That could possibly be said of any long-distance trail, but on this north coast the terrain ranges from the flat polders of the Bay of Mont St-Michel to

the 70m high red cliffs of Cap Fréhel, and the even wilder slopes of Beg an Fry in Finistère. The whole route is peppered with unspoilt fishing villages – but there are also the fashionable resorts of Dinard and Perros-Guirec, the old towns like St-Malo, Tréguier and Morlaix, as well as the commercial centre of St-Brieuc. Beaches range from perfect horseshoes of fine white sand to shingly coves with pebbles rattled by the waves, seascapes change from open ocean to calm estuary, and the rock mutates through glowing red sandstone to sombre deep blue granite.

Added to this heady mixture are those elements that are essentially Breton – churches with open bell walls or latticed spires, ancient carved calvaries at the crossroads, menhirs and dolmens scattered across the land. Brittany is one of the seven oyster-producing areas of France and the flat-bottomed boats and mesh sacks of oysters are omnipresent. So too are the seafood restaurants, and although you may not feel like one of those magnificent seafood platters every night, moules-frites eaten overlooking the sea can be a very acceptable alternative.

Walking the entire route for this book has been an unforgettable experience. I had walked many sections previously, but feeling the whole evolve in sequence was magical. At the end of the day, I must thank my husband Eric, who not only walked with me, but also met me, ferried me, carried the heavier pack and generally took charge of operations. Mine was the easy part! I hope that if you, too, are inspired to set foot on this path, you will enjoy it as much as we have. Good luck on your journey!

Judy Smith

1. Mont St-Michel - Cancale

Bay of Mont St-Michel

43 kms

For anyone contemplating the entire Brittany Coastal Path, Mont St-Michel makes a suitably prestigious starting point - albeit that the Mont is in Normandy! Bretons blame this latter fact on the vagaries of the River Couesnon, traditionally the border between the two regions, whose course has altered over the years. Be that as it may, today's boundary is well west of the river and if you are setting out on the path you won't be able to say that you are in Brittany for certain until you have walked almost 12kms.

After crossing the causeway from Mont St-Michel, most of this section is on the dyke that holds back the sea from the cultivated polder. This interface of land and sea is a magical place of high-arching skies and wide horizons. The flat arable fields on one side of the dyke are balanced on the other by sheep-grazed marshes that reach far out into the muddy sea. The familiar silhouette of Mont St-Michel grows ever distant, and in the bay itself you can keep an eye on the tide that, according to Victor Hugo, 'comes in like a galloping horse'. Cancale is reached via the oyster port of La Houle, and you must surely promise yourself a plateful at one of the many restaurants along the seafront or in the town.

MONT ST-MICHEL

In prehistoric times the Bay of Mont St-Michel was dry land, and the rock on which town and abbey now stand was a bare lump of granite that had resisted erosion better than the surrounding terrain. The sea subsequently invaded, and the story goes that in 708, St-Aubert, the Bishop of Avranches, had a dream in which the archangel Michael asked that he build a church upon this rock that was now an island. Being not given to hard work, Aubert promptly put the dream out of his mind, but it recurred night after night - and the archangel finally increased the pressure by putting a burning finger through the saint's skull. (The said skull can be seen at the church of St-Gervais in Avranches, and you may be forgiven for thinking that the archangel had podgy fingers!) A small oratory was duly built, and was much extended on the arrival of Benedictine monks some 200 years later. Hard on their heels came the pilgrims. This enigmatic site drew the faithful from far and wide - for some British pilgrims it also became a desirable halt on the road to Santiago de Compostella. The Revolution put an end to it all, and for many years the abbey was used as a prison, before a campaign for its rescue had it declared a historic monument in 1874.

Mont St-Michel is now a World Heritage site, it receives around 3.5 million visitors a year, and is the most visited attraction in France outside Paris. If you can steer clear of the throng (perhaps come in January) there are fine views to be had of the Bay, the rock of Tombelaine to the north and the surrounding coastline. The austere abbey itself is reached by several steep flights of steps, and yet more legwork is needed for the labyrinthine tour of its empty rooms, but for those who come to this site, the visit is surely almost obligatory.

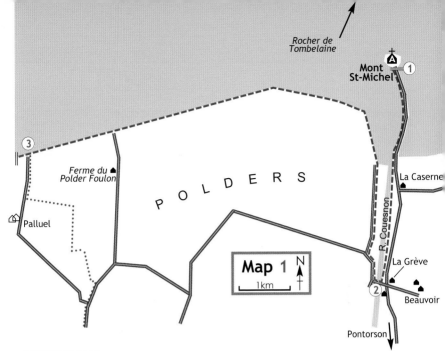

DIRECTIONS

1/1 Leave Mont St-Michel on path beside causeway (or if preferred, grassy path along bottom of dyke) • **Do not be tempted to cross over lock gates at mouth of R. Couesnon (dangerous and forbidden), but discipline yourself to continue for a further 2km along the dyke** • Pass through La Caserne and **CA** to hamlet of La Grève

1/2 At La Grève go **R** over Pont de Beauvoir (**across the Couesnon**) • Over bridge, turn **R** on road, then first **R** (signed St-Joseph) • At end of road, go through wooden gate to **CA** on dyke, soon bending **L** • **There are fine views of Mont St-Michel and the rock of Tombelaine behind**

1/3 ALTERNATIVE: Some 10km on from bridge, after road going to farm of Polder Foulon, the path reaches a junction with the road to Palluel. Here a waymarked alternative route turns off inland, passing through Roz-sur-Couesnon, Dol-de-Bretagne and Mont Dol (a similar granite rock to that of Mont St-Michel) before rejoining coastal path just before Hirel (see Map 3)

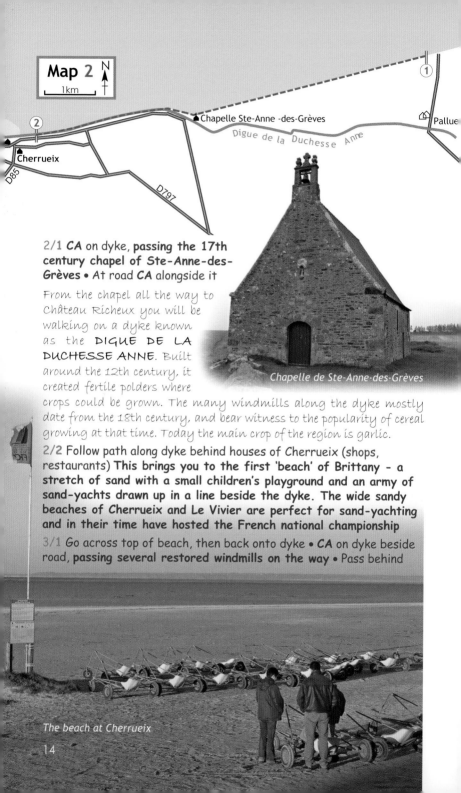

Map 2

N

1km

①

② Chapelle Ste-Anne -des-Grèves

Pallue

Digue de la Duchesse Anne

Cherrueix

D85

D797

2/1 CA on dyke, passing the 17th century chapel of Ste-Anne-des-Grèves • At road CA alongside it

From the chapel all the way to Château Richeux you will be walking on a dyke known as the **DIGUE DE LA DUCHESSE ANNE**. Built around the 12th century, it created fertile polders where

Chapelle de Ste-Anne-des-Grèves

crops could be grown. The many windmills along the dyke mostly date from the 18th century, and bear witness to the popularity of cereal growing at that time. Today the main crop of the region is garlic.

2/2 Follow path along dyke behind houses of Cherrueix (shops, restaurants) This brings you to the first 'beach' of Brittany - a stretch of sand with a small children's playground and an army of sand-yachts drawn up in a line beside the dyke. The wide sandy beaches of Cherrueix and Le Vivier are perfect for sand-yachting and in their time have hosted the French national championship

3/1 Go across top of beach, then back onto dyke • CA on dyke beside road, passing several restored windmills on the way • Pass behind

The beach at Cherrueix

houses of La Larronnière and **CA** to Le Vivier-sur-Mer • **The first buildings of Le Vivier are the huge dark sheds of the Maison de la Baie, an enterprise offering visitors a** closer look at the Bay and the procedures involved in mussel culture (mytiliculture)

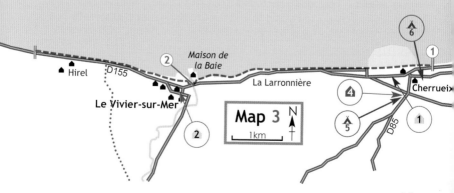

Maison de la Baie organises trips to the mussel beds

3/2 Beside Maison de la Baie, cross river on road (D155) and immediately turn **R** into port area • Walk past all boats and tractors, then turn **L** on path alongside small field to return to dyke (**After 1km the inland variant of the path rejoins this coastal route**) • Follow dyke beside D155 to Hirel (restaurant)

Hirel · D155 · Maison de la Baie · La Larronnière · Le Vivier-sur-Mer · Cherrueix · D85

Map 3 N 1km

MUSSEL FARMING

Mussels were certainly known to the Romans, who regarded them as delicacies for special occasions, but there is no record of cultivation before the 13th century. Today several methods of mussel culture exist, but in Normandy and Brittany they are generally grown on huge oak stakes 6-8m tall, arranged in 'bouchots', spaced to allow the passage of a flat-bottomed boat.

In early spring, when the sea temperature begins to rise, these posts are driven in along the low-tide mark, and ropes are tied tightly between them to form a sort of grill. Mussels release their minuscule larvae in millions at this time of year, and they are carried in by the tides to attach themselves to the ropes. It takes a further six weeks or so before they are visible to the naked eye.

In early summer, with the young mussels just a centimetre or so across, the ropes are cut from the posts and wound around them instead. These young mussels are placed farthest from the shore, and are subsequently moved inland as they grow. The mussels are finally harvested by hand or by machine at around 18 - 24 months of age.

The Bay of St-Michel is the most important mussel farming area in France, yielding 1/6 of the national production.

MYTILICULTURE ET DECOUVERTE
BAIE DU MONT SAINT MICHEL
VISITE

4/1 **CA** along dyke to St-Benoit-des-Ondes

4/2 **Leaving St-Benoit, the path on the dyke comes to an end where the vegetation is no longer cut back. You could stay on the dyke and struggle through the long grass, but the marked path goes inland** • Turn down road on **L** (rue de la Baie), then up first road on **R** (Pont Benoit) to return to D155 • Cross this road diagonally **L**, taking rough road towards more mussel sheds • Bear **L** in front of them (**Château Richeux peeps through the trees on the cliff ahead**) • At end of rough road **CA** on path, around shore below château, to a pretty beach • Leave beach on wooden ladder to return to coastal path, now running behind wide sweep of sand, then climbing to cliffs

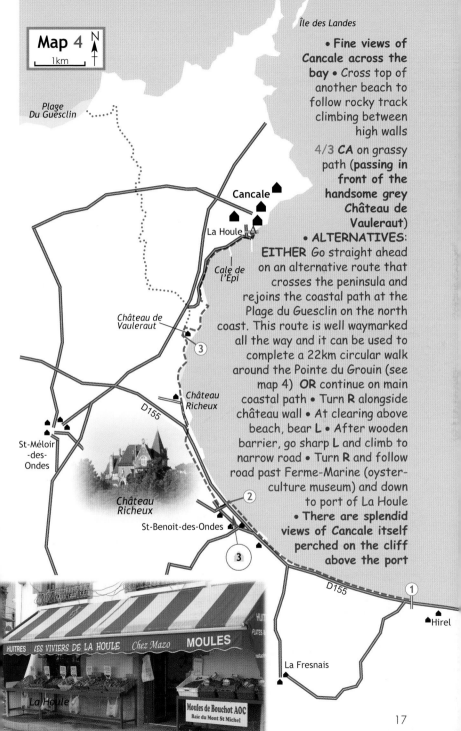

Pointe du Grouin

Île des Landes

Map 4 N

1km

Plage Du Guesclin

Cancale

La Houle

Cale de l'Epi

Château de Vauleraut

③

Château Richeux

D155

St-Méloir -des- Ondes

Château Richeux

②

St-Benoit-des-Ondes

③

D155

①

Hirel

La Fresnais

LES VIVIERS DE LA HOULE *Chez Mazo* **MOULES**

HUITRES

La Houle

Moules de Bouchot AOC
Baie du Mont St Michel

• **Fine views of Cancale across the bay** • Cross top of another beach to follow rocky track climbing between high walls

4/3 **CA** on grassy path (**passing in front of the handsome grey Château de Vauleraut**) • **ALTERNATIVES: EITHER** Go straight ahead on an alternative route that crosses the peninsula and rejoins the coastal path at the Plage du Guesclin on the north coast. This route is well waymarked all the way and it can be used to complete a 22km circular walk around the Pointe du Grouin (see map 4) **OR** continue on main coastal path • Turn **R** alongside château wall • At clearing above beach, bear **L** • After wooden barrier, go sharp **L** and climb to narrow road • Turn **R** and follow road past Ferme-Marine (oyster-culture museum) and down to port of La Houle • **There are splendid views of Cancale itself perched on the cliff above the port**

17

La Houle and the Cale de l'Épi, Cancale beyond

• At bottom of hill, **CA** along promenade **with its many shellfish stalls and restaurants**

The first of the two breakwaters at la Houle has a rather curious appearance. Constructed in 1837, its many arches were designed to let the current pass through without resultant silting, and it was later extended to allow boats to dock. Now restored (although the arches are blocked with sand), this Cale de l'épi (dock-breakwater) is unique in France.

• At roundabout near second breakwater, **CA** through barrier • 100m double back **L** on path leading up to monument on top of hill • **Directly below are Cancale's famous oyster beds, clearly visible at low tide**

Cancale's oyster beds

1. PRACTICAL INFORMATION

SHOPS & SERVICES
- Mont St-Michel TO 02 33 60 14 30 www.ot-montsaintmichel.com

• La Grève	• Cherrueix
• Le Vivier-sur-Mer	• Hirel
• St-Benoit-des-Ondes	• La Houle

- Cancale TO 02 99 89 63 72 www.cancale-tourisme.fr

See also: www.ville-cancale.fr • www.pays-de-dol.com

ACCOMMODATION

Chambres d'Hôte
1. La Renardière (200m) 21 rue du Lion d'Or, 35120 Cherrueix
   06 78 71 55 14 www.cotemer-cotejardin.com
2. La Chatonnière des Müller-Langlais (200m) 34 rue de Dol, 35960 Le
   Vivier-sur-Mer 02 99 48 97 74 www.vivier.biz
3. Mme Théault (on route) 60 rue du Bord de Mer, 35114 St-Benoit-des-
   Ondes 02 99 58 76 90 http://faceauxflots.site.voila.fr

Gîte d'étape
4. Gîte d'étape de l'Aumone (500m) 35120 Cherrueix 02 99 48 97 28

Camping
5. Camping de l'Aumone (500m) 35120 Cherrueix 02 99 48 95 11
   www.camping-de-laumone.com Open mid-June to mid-September
6. Camping Le Tenzor de la Baie (300m) 10 bis rue Théophile Blin,
   35120 Cherrueix 02 99 48 98 13 www.le-tenzor-de-la-baie.com
   Open late March to early October

TRANSPORT
Bus services: St-Malo - Cancale, *also* St-Malo - St-Benoit-des-Ondes -
   Hirel www.ksma.fr
   St-Malo - Dol-de-Bretagne - Pontorson - Mont St-Michel
   www.lescourriersbretons.com
   Pontorson - Mont St-Michel www.mobi50.com
Taxi: Taxi de la Grève 02 99 48 81 90 Le Vivier-sur-Mer
   Taxi de la Baie 02 99 89 87 20 Cancale
   Taxi Cancale 02 99 89 73 90 Cancale

OTHER WALKS
This flat area may not be the best for circular walks, but nevertheless
the Office de Tourisme in Dol-de-Bretagne (www.pays-de-dol.com) can
offer you details of several interesting well-waymarked circuits, some
incorporating sections of the coastal path.

An unaccompanied walk out into the bay is not advisable: contact the
Maison de la Baie at Le Vivier. They organise walks led by suitably
informed and equipped guides, as well as train rides to the mussel beds.
Tel. 02 99 48 84 38 (www.maison-baie.com)

Oysters at Cancale

SHELLFISH

Oysters, mussels, clams, cockles, winkles, whelks, scallops, lobsters, crabs – the north coast of Brittany is teeming with them all, and there is no way you can come to Brittany without sampling a seafood platter. It would be tantamount to holidaying in Cornwall and never indulging in a Cornish pastie – unthinkable! And besides, in walking this path you will appreciate all the effort that has gone into your meal.

Pride of place must, of course, go to the oysters. France is undoubtedly the oyster-centre of Europe and the French love oysters. 90% of the production are eaten at home – and amazingly, half of those slip down in the week between Christmas and New Year! Today's prices reflect both their culinary esteem and the time that has gone into producing them, but things were not always so. The Romans cultivated oysters, and the Greeks swore by their aphrodisiac powers, but in the Middle Ages, wild oysters were simply free food for peasants living near the coast. It was only when it became possible to transport oysters inland that cultivation began in earnest - and oysters found themselves in some high places. Louis XIV had them regularly delivered to Versailles for his breakfast and Napoleon always downed a dozen or more before a major battle. From time to time there have been troubles with the oyster business when viruses have decimated stock, but it has always been replenished and today it is mostly the thick-shelled Pacific (or Japanese) oysters that are grown. That said, the native Brittany flat oysters (Bélons) are generally considered to have a better flavour, and are the pride of Cancale.

Oysters are now mostly bred in controlled circumstances (maybe in southern Brittany or the Marennes-Oléron basin) and the young spat then transported to be reared elsewhere. Placed in mesh sacks, they are laid out on long racks raised off the sea bed to protect them from predators. They grow by filtering plankton, and when the tide allows the flat boats access, they are

Oysters in mesh sacks

turned and tended carefully. It is some 4 years before oysters can be harvested and they then need to be washed carefully and perhaps spend a spell in a clearing tank before heading for the table.

Mussels are the only other shellfish that are cultivated on this coast, and the buchots, forests of thick black stakes poking through the shallow water are a common site, particularly in the Bays of La Fresnaye and St-Brieuc. The annual cycle starts when sea temperatures begin to rise in early spring – ropes are tied between the stakes and the millions of mussel larvae released at this time fasten themselves on. There they grow for the next few weeks, but

Buchots for mussel cultivation

when they are big enough to be seen with the naked eye, the ropes are cut loose and wound around the stakes. 18 months or so later the mussels can be harvested, a process once done by hand, but now usually by special machine.

Scallops have much the same history as oysters in that they were once everyman's food. But in the Bay of St-Brieuc, scallops are fished, not farmed, and at the height of their new-found celebrity in the 70s, the population of scallops in the bay of St-Brieuc was almost entirely wiped out. Strict regulations now govern both the mesh of the dragnet and the hours that may be spent on scallop fishing, and boats that do this in the permitted winter months often take on another role for the summer. Erquy and St-Quay-Portrieux are the main centres for scallop fishing in Brittany, but scallops are also found along the shores of Galicia in north-west Spain. It was their prevalence here that led to them being adopted as the emblem of the pilgrims making their way to the shrine of St-James in Santiago de Compostella – hence their

French name, Coquilles St-Jacques.

Coquille St-Jacques

Other shellfish are the domain of the scavengers, and although they may be gathered professionally, at low tide in the estuaries you may see whole families out with their nets and buckets. St-Jacut is probably the best place to head for if you would like to join them, but there as everywhere, shellfishing is strictly regulated and it pays to ask at the Tourist Office first. Clams (palourdes) and cockles (cocques) can be found on or just under the wet sand, while winkles (bigorneaux) live on algae-covered rocks. Whelks (bulots) are predators that can be found anywhere – and they are well removed as their carnivorous instincts are so strong that they will bore into the shells of oysters and scallops.

Usually included with the shellfish are the crustaceans, lobsters (homards), Dublin Bay prawns (langoustines), brown crabs (tourteaux) and spider crabs (araignées). Where once north Breton fishermen headed for the cod fields of Iceland or Newfoundland, it is now inshore fishing for these delicacies that gives them their livelihood. The little town of Loguivy to the north of Paimpol is very proud of its 'blue lobster' – but this particular specimen is also found elsewhere along this coast. Lobsters and crabs are usually kept in tanks before sale and ports like le Diben on the Rade de Morlaix take great pleasure in displaying the live contents of a seafood platter.

Brittany is so proud of its seafood that restaurateurs have now drawn up a charter to define an authentic Breton Plateau de Fruits de Mer. Apparently it must contain at least 3 different crustaceans and 3 shellfish, all served on a bed of seaweed. A treat not to be missed!

gathering shellfish

2. Cancale-St-Malo

Clos Poulet

33 kms

This is a wonderfully attractive section, with the pine-shaded path first winding its sheltered way along cliffs high above a sea scattered with rocky islands. The luxurious vegetation is gradually left behind, and the path becomes more undulating and demanding as it heads for the long craggy outcrop of the Pointe du Grouin. This is the place to pause and take in the view. By contrast the north coast is clad in an open moorland of gorse and heather, with rocky headlands interspersed by bays of fine white sand. At Rothéneuf bizarre sculptures decorate the cliffs and you could divert to visit the home of 16th century explorer Jacques Cartier before pressing on to St-Malo. The great maritime city is best reached by walking barefoot along the Grande Plage, from which there are fine views of the old walled town.

CANCALE AND THE OYSTER INDUSTRY

There is nothing new or exotic about eating oysters. In the Middle Ages, oysters were gathered wild on the coasts of both Britain and France and were a staple food for those living near the sea. When it became possible to transport the oysters inland, farming, formerly practised only by the Romans, began anew.

The bay around Cancale is an ideal location for oyster-farming on account of its shallow protected waters, rich in specially-beneficial plankton - nevertheless, the young oysters are not born here. The local population of oysters was completely wiped out by a mysterious disease in 1920, and since then the oyster spats have always been imported from the south of Brittany. Once on the site they are grown on in mesh containers laid out in rectangular beds. Tended regularly by the farmers, they take some 4 years to reach maturity, and need careful washing before they can be offered to the public. On the stalls of Cancale you will find various types of oyster - native flat bélons, thick-shelled ridged creusés originating from Japanese stock, and the enormous and consequently expensive pieds de cheval (horse's hooves). Eat them fresh, with lemon juice, crusty bread and white wine - but amateurs should beware the sharp knives needed to open them. Perhaps repair to one of the many quayside restaurants instead!

Alfresco lunch by the oyster beds

DIRECTIONS

5/1 Before reaching monument on top of hill, turn off **R** on Chemin de Ronde and **CA** • **This fine balcony path has a bird's eye view of the oyster beds below and rocky islands out to sea** • At fork bear **R** twice, descend to back of beach, then climb again • **CA** on increasingly undulating path round wooded Pointe de la Chaîne • **Out to sea two islands can be seen - the second has a late 18th century fort - while ahead there are distant views of the Pointe du Grouin** • Briefly emerging on road, bear off **R** again, and after further winding along cliffs, descend to beach at Port Briac • Cross **P** and climb long

Port Briac

flight of steps on opposite side • Still in woodland, **CA** along cliffs to Port Pican • **Here a stylish modern Youth Hostel, *Auberge de Jeunesse*, faces the bay** • Walk in front of youth hostel to rejoin coastal path and climb once more to cliffs

5/2 **CA** round Pointe du Chatry and gradually descend to seafront at Port Mer (restaurants) • **CA** past all the

Auberge de Jeunesse, Port Pican

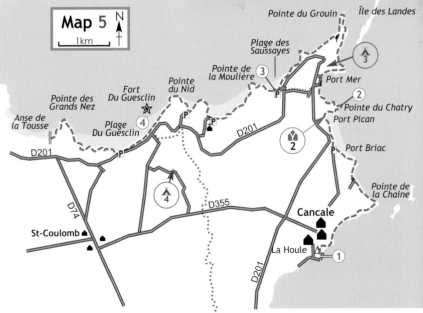

Map 5

N

1km

Pointe du Grouin
Île des Landes
Plage des Saussayes
Pointe de la Moulière ③
Port Mer
Pointe du Nid
Fort Du Guesclin
Pointe des Grands Nez
Anse de la Tousse
Plage Du Guesclin ④
D201
②
Pointe du Chatry
Port Pican
②
Port Briac
D201
Pointe de la Chaine
D74
④
D355
Cancale
St-Coulomb
La Houle ①
D201

Port Mer

appealing restaurants and begin to climb on tarmac road • 50m at left bend turn **R** onto coastal path • Pass old German blockhouses before reaching Pointe de Barbe Brulée • Skirt large campsite • **CA** below former signalling station, following path to Pointe du Grouin • From here, walk back past signalling station into its P and take path on **R** • Follow across rough moorland up to road, but descend again into bracken • **CA** to skirt P above beach, Plage des Saussayes

POINTE DU GROUIN

The whole of the Pointe du Grouin is a nature reserve and you are asked to keep to the paths to reduce erosion and preserve the fragile vegetation. The views are magnificent and the ceramic toposcope points out every detail. If the weather is reasonable you should at least be able to pick out the dark shapes of the Îles Chausey to the north, the white houses of Granville on the Normandy coast, and the familiar silhouette of Mont St-Michel far across the bay. Nearer at hand, the long bare outcrop to the east of the Point is the Île des Landes, an ornithological reserve, home to families of gulls, cormorants, shelducks, oyster-catchers and more. The 'Vieille Rivière' channel between Point and island is renowned for its treacherous currents, generated by the dramatic swings of tide here. With an amplitude of more than 13 metres, the Pointe de Grouin boasts the highest rise of tide in Europe. The white signalling station on its summit is no longer in use, its role having been usurped by those with more up-to-date technology in 1999.

Plage des Saussayes

5/3 Follow downhill across beach access road • **CA** under thick vegetation on opposite side • Climb again, following around deep cleft in rock, to Pointe de la Moulière • **From these vertiginous heights the view opens up with the wide golden arc of the Plage du Verger ahead** • Descend to **TJ** of paths, turn **R** to reach sandy track along back of beach • At clearing beneath pine trees, turn **R** and **CA** on track to P

From the beach car park, a diversion of some 150m up the access road will bring you to the grey stone Chapelle du Verger. This photogenic chapel was built in 1869, although it is known that there has been a chapel on this site since the 10th century.

• Where access road goes **L** from P, take path on **R**, climbing under pine trees (**Soon there is a fine view back across the bay to the Pointe du Grouin**) • Continue down to little beach and P

The grey building on the clifftop just above you may look like another chapel but it is actually a Corps de Garde, a customs officers' guardroom, built here in the 17th century. The 'belfry' at one end is a small watch tower.

• **CA** across head of beach on obvious path • Follow to prominent Pointe du Nid, then descend to Plage du Guesclin

Just offshore, the **Fort du Guesclin** *crowns a rocky islet. The original fort here was built in the 12th century by the De Guesclin family (ancestors of the renowned Bertrand du Guesclin, military commander of Hundred Years War fame). The ramparts you see today are the result of endeavours to defend the coast against English invasion in 1758.*

A road on the L here is the end of the alternative route from Vauléraut, just south of Cancale (see p.17)

5/4 CA behind Plage du Guesclin, then join road at far end • Past P take coastal path on **R** • Follow this tortuous path to Pointe des Grands Nez • Continue down to glorious sands of Anse de la Touesse

ANSE DE LA TOUESSE This lovely bay is divided centrally by a high rocky outcrop. The desirable property overlooking the first part of the bay is Roz Ven, once the home of famous French writer Colette, and the setting for her romantic novel *Le Blé en Herbe* (1923).

6/1 Cross sand and climb steep wooden staircase to top of dividing rocky promontory • Follow path skirting fence of Roz Ven, then **CA** through dunes above beach • At far end turn **L** (**the very beautiful Plage du Port is on the R**) • Follow path **R** and **CA** around lofty Pointe

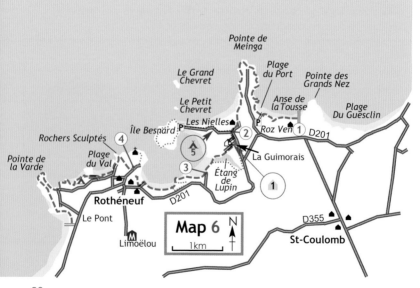

Pointe de Meinga

de Meinga • **The western side of the headland has views across the islands of Le Grand and Le Petit Chevet, the larger Île Besnard, and the fine sweep of sand connecting it to the mainland** • Reaching beach level, path soon becomes access road to Ferme des Nielles • Continue on road to junction just past farm

6/2 **DIVERSION** (4km): turn **R** for optional diversion to Île Besnard, with its own attractive coastal path, then return to this point

• **MAIN ROUTE:** turn **L** and continue to village of la Guimorais

• **ALTERNATIVES**: Here a notice painted on a concrete post offers a choice – at low tide you can take a short-cut across an estuary known as the Étang de Lupin, at high tide you must keep on the road a little farther

Low tide option: Turn **R** in village and walk down to quay • Turn **R** and pick your way (often muddy) along bank of estuary to crumbling seaweed covered dyke passable only at low water • On far side, go **R** across beach to access road

Étang de Lupin (low-tide route)

High tide option: (This may be preferable whatever the tide!) CA through village to meet main road • Turn **R** along it 150m • Turn **R** on signed path plunging through pine trees • Continue across wall at head of estuary • On far side turn **R** along field edge • 400m go through hedge on **R** to descend to beach beside estuary • Walk **L** along beach to access road

6/3 Just up access road, pick up coastal path again on **R** • Skirt field

Rothéneuf

and **CA** under pine trees of Île Esnau promontory • **CA** across beach to rocks before beach and harbour at Rothéneuf (**very high tide may require deviation via main road to arrive at same point**) • From little beach at Rothéneuf, walk up access road, then take first narrow road on **R** between walls • 200m follow **L**, then **R** to reach another tarmac road

6/4 **DIVERSION**(1km): From here, turn **R** along road 70m, then **L** on path to reach the pretty mariners' chapel of Notre Dame des Flots overlooking the islands • Return same way (onward path gets lost along cliff) and follow main route

MAIN ROUTE: turn **L** on tarmac road, then immediately **R** to arrive at the Rochers Sculptés

ROTHÉNEUF, now a suburb of St-Malo, has plenty of interest. The curious Rochers Sculptés are passed on the coastal path (see opposite) but a little diversion is necessary to take in Rothéneuf's other claim to fame. **Jacques Cartier**, who discovered Canada in 1534, was born in the village, and later in life lived at the Manoir de Limoëlou (1km south). Rooms at the Manoir have been restored as in his time and audio-visual presentations offer an insight into his voyages. To reach the Manoir, walk to the centre of Rothéneuf and follow the signs.

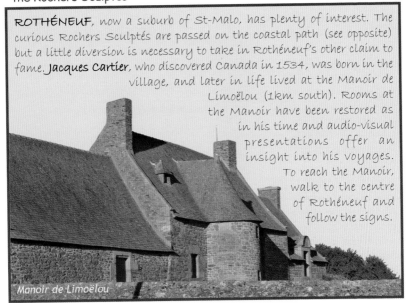

Manoir de Limoëlou

ROCHERS SCULPTÉS

These extraordinary rock carvings were made by retired priest Abbé Fouré over a period of some 25 years at the end of the 19th century. More than 300 individual figures adorn the cliff face. Infamous local pirates and corsairs rub shoulders with saints and grotesque figures from the underworld, all of them poised startlingly above an azure sea.

• Take track on **L** of Rochers Sculptés, around headland to road down to Plage du Val, finally down flight of steps on **R** • Cross beach either on sand or esplanade • Turn **L** to rejoin road, going **R** along it • Turn immediately **R** on Avenue du Nicet • Follow uphill to end (including little bend **R** then **L**) • At entrance to Camping du Nicet go through gate, then turn sharp **R** to path along cliff on outside of campsite fence • Follow 800m to road, then head off **R** again to circumnavigate Pointe de la Varde (**a headland that is rather less attractive on account of its German blockhaus remains**) • Follow steps down to concrete walkway leading to beach at le Pont

Plage du Pont

Porte St-Vincent, St-Malo

7/1 Once on the Plage du Pont, the fortifications of St-Malo can clearly be seen at the extremity of the bay

ALTERNATIVES: Option 1. Easiest way to reach citadel is to continue across the sand, passing from Plage du Pont to Plage du Minihic, then Grande Plage of St-Malo. One or two low rocky outcrops must be negotiated on the way

Option 2. (Should option 1 not appeal – or if tide is very high) CA on roads just inland and above beach, or even catch a bus.

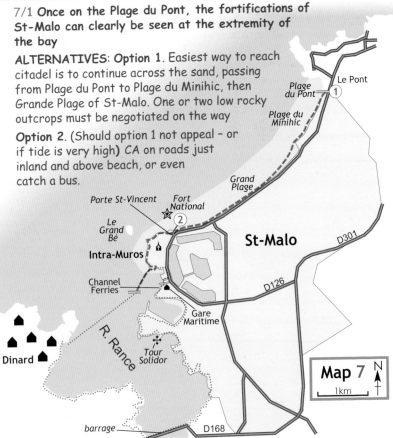

Le Pont

Plage du Pont ①

Plage du Minihic

Grand Plage

Porte St-Vincent

Fort National ②

Le Grand Bé

Intra-Muros

Channel Ferries

Gare Maritime

Tour Solidor

St-Malo

D301

D126

R. Rance

Dinard

barrage

D168

Map 7 N

1km

ST-MALO

St-Malo derives its name from the Welsh monk Mac Low, who arrived here in the 6th century and established his bishopric in that part of the town known as Aleth. In subsequent years the settlement moved to a nearby island, and acquired fortifications. Thriving on seafaring expeditions and trade with foreign lands, in 1590 St-Malo declared itself an independent republic. Its citizens defiantly took up the motto Ni François, ni Breton, Malouin suis (I am neither French nor Breton, but a man of St-Malo), but the independence lasted a mere 4 years. A century or so later, Vauban was called in to enlarge the city and reinforce its ramparts, thus creating the walled city (Intra Muros) we know today.

St-Malo may have begun as a religious foundation but over the centuries it acquired a very different reputation. Conveniently positioned at the mouth of the Rance and facing the Channel, it became the haunt of pirates and their 'legalised' version, the corsairs, who actually received a permit from the king to prey on foreign ships. The most feared of the corsairs, one Robert Surcouf, is commemorated by a bronze statue on the town walls. His brief reign of terror left him able to retire at the age of 36, a very rich man indeed!

Today most visitors to St-Malo head for Intra Muros, and its narrow streets are often crowded. The cathedral of St-Vincent with its fine stained glass windows is tucked in among old buildings of many storeys, all of them jostling for the limited space. And yet this city is not so old! Amazingly about 80% of what you see is a reconstruction, a sensitive recreation of the old St-Malo that was almost destroyed in the liberation battles of August 1944. The granite ramparts survived, and must be walked for the seaward view. To the east a low island is capped by Vauban's Fort National, while to the west the grassy Île du Grand Bé is home to the unmarked tomb of writer-politician Chateaubriand. The causeways to both islands, passable only at low tide, add to their attraction.

Robert Surcouf

7/2 Whatever route, the destination is the same – Porte St-Vincent, the main gateway to Intra Muros, the most fascinating part of St-Malo

ALTERNATIVES: From St-Malo it is necessary to cross the Rance to get to Dinard on the opposite bank and the simplest way to do this is to take the Navette.

Option 1. The Navette leaves from the jetty (embarcadère) at the south-west corner of Intra Muros, so you could take a walk along the ramparts to get there. If the Navette should not be running (winter), there is a private *Taxi de la mer* that operates all year round – see below for details.

Option 2. Take the bus to Dinard.

Option 3. A long detour south to cross the Rance on the Barrage. This route is mostly waymarked (particularly on the Dinard side) but you will have to make your own way through St-Malo. The recommended route crosses in front of the car ferry and then skirts the Plage des Sablons, rounds the promontory of Aleth and passes the Tour Solidor before taking to such paths and minor roads as most nearly border the coast.

In taking this long route there is the opportunity to visit the Usine Marémotrice de la Rance, the tidal power station on the Barrage that generates 8% of Brittany's electricity. Now more than 40 years old this power station is still unique in Europe and takes advantage of the exceptionally high rise of tide here.

Once across the Rance on the Barrage, turn sharp **R** (do not go up the hill) to pick up the well-marked coastal path climbing steps up the cliff. It now skirts one of the most scenic coastlines in Brittany to reach the ferry terminal at Dinard, and the continuation of the coastal path.

The ramparts, Intra-Muros, St-Malo

2. PRACTICAL INFORMATION

SHOPS & SERVICES

- **Cancale** TO 02 99 89 63 72 www.cancale-tourisme.fr Mkt Sun
- **St-Coulomb** TO 02 99 89 09 00 (May - Sept) www.saintcoulomb.com
- **St-Malo** TO 08 25 13 52 00 www.saint-malo-tourisme.com
  Mkt (Intra-Muros) Fri

ACCOMMODATION

Chambres d'hôte

1. M&Mme Sorre (on route) Chapijemi, 3 Impasse du Moulin de la Mer, La Guimorais, 35350 St-Coulomb 02 99 89 07 03

Dormitory

2. Auberge de Jeunesse (on route) Port Pican, 35260 Cancale 02 99 89 62 62 www.hihostels.com (70 beds, rooms for 1 - 6 persons)

Camping

3. Camping Port Mer Plage (on route) 32 Avenue de la Côte d'Émeraude, 35260 Cancale 02 99 89 63 17 www.location-mer-bretagne.com
4. Camping du Guesclin (800m) Tannée, 35350 St-Coulomb 02 99 89 03 24 www.campingduguesclin.com
5. Camping Les Chevrets (200m) La Guimorais, 35350 St-Coulomb 02 99 89 01 90 www.campingdeschevrets.fr

TRANSPORT

Bus services: Saint-Malo – St-Coulomb – Cancale www.ksma.fr

Navette: Vedettes de St-Malo (10 minute ferry trip St-Malo to Dinard, April to Sept only) 02 23 18 02 04 www.vedettes-saintmalo.com

Taxi de la Mer (Boat taxi St-Malo to Dinard, all year) 06 07 60 03 00 / 06 84 34 95 64

Taxi: Allo Taxis Malouins 02 99 81 30 30 St-Malo

OTHER WALKS

Pointe de Grouin offers several possibilities for circular walks:

For a 6km circuit, start at Port Mer, walk round to Plage des Saussayes, then cut back across the headland on the Rue des Tintiaux, crossing the main road to return to the seafront at Port Mer. (See Map 5)

A more substantial 22km circuit starting from Vauléraut, around Pointe du Grouin to Plage du Guesclin, returning on the GR34a is well-waymarked and much quicker than you might think, passing first through the attractive wooded valley of the Moulin Esnoux and continuing on broad tracks across farm land. (See p.17 and Maps 4 & 5)

Rochers sculptés, Rothéneuf

The 12km circuit of the Rance estuary. (See previous page, **Option 3**)

Lapwings in the Bay of St-Brieuc

BIRDWATCHING

The north coast of Brittany is an ornithologist's paradise. All those long sheltered bays that transform to vast mudflats at low tide provide perfect winter quarters for thousands of ducks, geese and waders that arrive from the north. Being on the axis of migration from northern Europe to Africa, there are also those who make these shores their stopping-off point, a place to rest and refuel before carrying on with their journey. And in summertime, when the mudflats go quiet, the more remote cliffs and all the offshore reefs and islands come alive with nesting seabirds.

The largest bay of all on this coast, the Bay of St-Brieuc, has been a designated nature reserve since 1998. The reserve has many constituents, but without doubt the most important is the birdlife. The tide goes out more than 7km here – and when the tide goes out, the waders move in, striding across the mud and thrusting their long beaks beneath the surface. Flocks of oyster-catchers and lapwings are joined by curlews, dunlins, sandpipers, plovers and lots more as they follow the receding waters in their search for food. The lives of these birds are governed by the state of the tide – they sleep when it is in and eat when it is out, throughout the 24-hour day.

Common Sandpiper

The season for the waders is between October and March, and of course they are best observed at low tide. Ducks and geese also feed in the intertidal zones

Brent Geese

but are frequently seen on the waters at high tide. Flocks of dark Brent Geese are a common sight, as are the more colourful mallards, shelduck and wigeon. Their winter season in the bay is generally shorter – perhaps between November and February – after which they move inland or north for the summer.

Black-headed Gull in winter plumage

Herring Gull

All the birds in the reserve can equally well be found anywhere else along this coast and if you are taking a winter ramble you are pretty sure to spot some of them. But for more information it is worth making a visit to the Maison de la Baie in Hillion (open every day in July and August, otherwise Wednesday, Friday and Sunday afternoons). In addition to exhibitions of bird life, they can offer you a free identification chart and the use of a telescope trained permanently on the bay.

In spring, ornithological interest switches to the seabirds. The bay of St-Brieuc may be quiet, but the islands are welcoming arrivals for the nesting season. The reserve of the Île des Landes (off the Pointe de Grouin) has the largest colony of shags in Europe, while the Sept Îles reserve (off Perros-Guirec) is teeming with rarer birds

Little Egret

like guillemots, razorbills, gannets and puffins. In fact the gannets arrive rather early (maybe January) and stay till September. If these are your interest, your very first port of call should be the Centre Ornithologique on the Île Grande. The smart little building is packed with information,

Telescope at the Maison de la Baie, Hillion

and has a 'gannet corner' with a video link to their breeding site on the Île Rouzic, the farthest out of the Sept Îles.

Boat trips from Perros-Guirec take visitors out to the Sept Îles all year round, but the birds must be observed from the water. Only certain excursions land on the largest island, the Île aux Moines, and that is more to see the lighthouse than the birds.

At the end of the summer season, very few birds remain on the islands. Some like terns and petrels simply migrate south, but guillemots, gannets and puffins amazingly spend the winter on the wing, following their food across the oceans. Even more amazing are the adaptations they need for this life – special lightweight 'airy' bones and glands in the skull that filter excess salt from their food. These strange facts of avian life and a lot more are revealed at the Île Grande Centre Ornithologique, which also has something of a reputation as a bird hospital, and is well worth a visit.

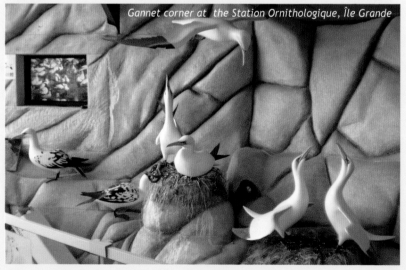
Gannet corner at the Station Ornithologique, Île Grande

3. Dinard - St-Cast
Le Côte d'Émeraude 1
55 kms

To begin with this is the most urban section of the whole coastal path, and yet it is also one of the most exciting. From fashionable Dinard, where Belle-Époque villas grace the cliffs, a succession of fine family-friendly beaches is broken at St-Lunaire by the long rocky Pointe du Décollé. Around the corner, the harbour of St-Briac is surely one of the prettiest spots in all Brittany. Sandy beaches briefly return before the path takes a wide sweep around the shallow Bay of Lancieux, filled not with sand but with red-tinged glassworts and other salt-loving plants. Continuing up the coast at St-Jacut, the flat expanses where sand-yachts race give way to more intimate coves of white sand, while at the Pointe du Chevet there are fine views of the idyllic Île des Hébihens, just out to sea. Subsequent highlights are the ruined castle of Gilles-de-Bretagne, the 'Ringing Stones' at le Guildo, and the resort of St-Cast with a monument on every headland.

DINARD AND THE BELLE-ÉPOQUE

Dinard was merely a small fishing village until the middle of the 19th century when merchants from St-Malo and wealthy middle-classes from both Britain and America started to build their villas here. No-one seems sure who arrived first, but very quickly Dinard became a fashionable resort and fine gardens with palm trees, mimosa and eucalyptus sprang up beside its sheltered beaches. Near the main beach, the Plage des Écluses, a theatre and a casino opened to provide night-time entertainment and when the new daring idea of sea-bathing took hold in Europe, Dinard was at the forefront of the scene. Even today handsome beach-huts ring the Plage des Écluses. Dubbed the 'Cannes of the North', Dinard has attracted some illustrious holiday-makers over the years, Winston Churchill, Picasso and Lawrence of Arabia among them. Most celebrated seems to be Alfred Hitchcock, who spent many summers here, and whose house in the film 'Psycho' was inspired by a villa on the cliffs. His statue with seagulls on his shoulders overlooks the Plage des Écluses, and commemorates a popular British Film Festival, held here in October every year. In recent years Dinard has acquired more family appeal, although events like golf championships, yacht races and tennis tournaments still fill the social calendar.

The coastal path around the Pointe de Moulinet (the Promenade du Clair de Lune) and its continuation on the Plage des Écluses give the best glimpse of Dinard in its Belle-Époque heyday.

Promenade du Clair de Lune

DIRECTIONS

8/1 From jetty (*embarcadère*) at Dinard, turn **R** to follow concrete walkway decked with flowers, past little beach, then under cliffs all the way around Pointe du Moulinet

This is the northern end of the Promenade du Clair de Lune (Moonlight Promenade), a raised path running south around the Baie du Prieuré. Softly-lit gardens and piped music in summertime add to its romantic atmosphere.

• On reaching Plage de l'Écluse, pass old sea-water swimming pool and its latter-day replacement and **CA** along back of beach beside long rows of beach-huts

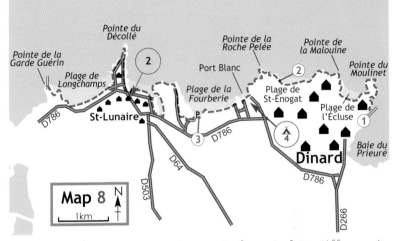

Looking across the beach, the villa on the far end of the cliffs opposite was the inspiration for Psycho.

• **CA** on walkway beneath cliffs of Pointe de la Malouine to arrive at last on sands at St-Énogat

8/2 Cross to middle of beach and climb flight of steps to modern thalassotherapy complex on cliff above • Turn **R** to skirt building and **CA** on coastal path to headland of la Roche Pelée • **Of the many islets to sea, the largest is the Île Cézembre** • Follow down to pass a pretty cove • Continue down to beach of Port Blanc • Leave this beach on its access road, walk up alongside campsite, then turn **R** and **R** again to return to Plage de la Fourberie • Walk across beach to first rocky outcrop and look for concrete steps in cliff leading under archway alongside white balustrade (This looks like a private entrance, but a waymark confirms the route) • Follow up between houses and cliff edge before turning **L** up log steps • Turn **R** and go ahead down to beach

8/3 From small **P**, take broad track going uphill

Walkway before Plage de St-Énogat

Pointe du Décollé

• Keep ahead (**the original coastal path on the R has been barred off due to erosion**), and ignore **L** turn signed Circuit des Papillons • Pass between boulders and on to tarmac road • 30m, at end of hedge, turn **R** on path • Follow alongside field to tarmac road • Turn **R** and continue to end • *CA* on path • Follow **L** round headland at dramatic height before returning alongside estuary • At main road, turn **R** to cross head of estuary and *CA* towards St-Lunaire • Take first road on **R** • At **L** bend *CA* to seafront promenade, turn **L** under pine trees (**View of Pointe du Décollé from here**)

ST-LUNAIRE *A popular resort with handsome villas and fine beaches, it was apparently the winds and waves at St-Lunaire that inspired Debussey's composition of La Mer.*

• At end of promenade (**with the fine 19th century Grand Hotel on the left**), turn **L** up Rue de la Grève, then **R** and **R** again, signed Pointe du Décollé (**In this fashionable quarter of St-Lunaire, the villas almost rival those of Dinard**) • Bear **R** at end to Pointe du Décollé

POINTE DU DÉCOLLÉ *This long tongue of rock projecting into the sea offers coastal views from St-Malo in the east to St-Cast and Cap Fréhel in the west. At its end are the remains of a watchtower, and below the ruins, a rough path with worn steps drops down to a 'Fairy Cave'. Take great care if you contemplate this difficult descent and remember that the cave is only accessible at low tide.*

Pointe du Décollé

• Returning from Pointe du Décollé, bear **R** on road along west side of peninsula (**passing viewpoint of Rocher Napoléon on R**) • Just before main road, turn **R** (Boulevard de la Fontaine), then bear **R** to Plage de Longchamps • **CA** along promenade • At end take steps up cliff • At road, bear **R** on hedged path, then follow signs to climb to top of Pointe du Garde-Guérin (**Paths abound here, but all uphill ones lead to the summit**)

The Romans once had a temple on the Pointe de Garde-Guérin, and at 48m above the sea, it has always been a valuable look-out post. There is a particularly fine prospect to the west, across the beaches of St-Briac and the islands out to sea.

9/1 Descend from Point on grassy track, bear **R** to pass between golf course and beach • At **TJ**, go **L** (**R leads to a little headland**) • At small P take narrow concrete path down to beach • Walk across beach to access road, but do not take it, instead **CA** beside old blockhaus and bear **R** to skirt house on cliff • **CA** to

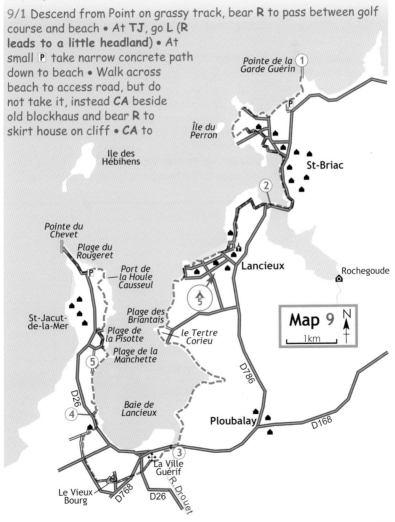

Looking west from Pointe de la Garde Guérin

road, follow **R** to end **(from here the way ahead to the Pointe de la Haye is private)** • Follow coastal path **L** alongside golf course • Past Île du Perron **(accessible at low tide)** turn sharply inland to reach first houses of St-Briac • At the end of the access road, turn **L** and almost immediately bear **R** • Take the next **R** again • Follow to **TJ** in front of big hedge • Turn **L** here, then **R** to reach St-Briac's attractive harbour • Continue **L** around harbour • At far end take alley to **R** of main road **(This old road leads up to the main D786)** • At D786 turn **R** downhill **(TO on left)** • Follow D786 alongside Frémur estuary and over bridge

ST-BRIAC-SUR-MER

St-Briac took its name from an Irish monk who arrived here in 548. Despite its scenic location at the mouth of the Frémur, it somehow never attained the fashionable status of other north coast resorts. It nevertheless attracted the impressionists of the 19th century, among them Émile Bernard, Paul Signac and Auguste Renoir. Today holiday makers come to enjoy St-Briac's nine beautiful beaches - and the view across its harbour to the headland where the Château of Nessay peeps above the trees is one to be found in many a tourist brochure.

Early morning on the beach at Lancieux

9/2 From end of bridge, bear **R** ahead and follow road into Lancieux (ignore signs on **R** – path is overgrown and merely parallels road) • In Lancieux (just before church) turn **R** on Rue Saint-Sieu • Follow **L**, then at junction bear **R** down to beach

LANCIEUX The celtic prefix 'lan' refers to a church or monastery – in this case, the monastery of Sieu, a disciple of St-Brieuc.

• Go onto beach and walk in front of Centre Nautique and beach huts • Continue past next access road and first rocky outcrop • From next section of beach take wide concrete steps up to Boulevard de la Mer • Turn **R** and follow **L** (**the marked path on the right passing through the picnic area simply skirts the Pointe de Lancieux on the far side of the houses and rejoins**) • At sharp lefthand bend inland, **CA** on pleasant path winding along cliffs to Plage des Briantais • Cross head of this beach to pick up coastal path again (It leaves from access road but is not easily spotted – as a secure alternative, climb up low rocky outcrop to reach obvious white wooden bridge above (coastal path crosses this bridge) • **CA** through vegetation on point known as

Baie de Lancieux

THE SCHORRE AND THE SLIKKE

'Schorre' and 'Slikke' are Dutch words, but are used throughout Europe to describe the characteristics of the salt marshes. The schorre is that part of the shallow bay that is covered only at the highest of tides. It is colonised by salt-loving plants, most notably purslanes and glassworts. Marsh Samphire is a glasswort that spreads like a thick carpet over the bay, colouring it red at certain times of the year. By contrast, the slikke is covered at every tide and supports almost no vegetation. This is the terrain beloved by wading birds who find molluscs and worms under the mud.

Le Tertre Corieu • Cross narrow tarmac road, bearing slightly **L** • **CA** on well-signed path beside shallow Baie de Lancieux • **CA** beside low dyke, follow round to D768 at head of bay

9/3 At D768, turn **R** to cross bridge over R. Drouet • On far side of bridge, take path on **L** • Follow **R, L** and **R** to skirt arable fields and come out on drive of Château de Ville-Guérif • Turn **L** down drive • Cross D26 onto path winding through woodland to D786 • Bear **L** • 30m at calvary fork **R** • Follow broad rough track to road in hamlet of Vieux-Bourg • Cross diagonally **R**, and follow **L**, finally taking broad grassy track between fields and under trees • At road, turn **R** • 600m at road **TJ, CA** on grassy track (superb views across the bay) • 475m at track **TJ** turn **R** • Follow sunken track, passing **R** of farmhouse (along back wall) down to main road D26 • Turn **L** along main road (with care)

Port de la Houle Causseul

9/4 200m take track on **R**, follow to emerge behind mussel cultivators premises and join road • Turn **L** and almost immediately **R**, along top of stone sea wall **above the schorre of the bay (see opposite)**

9/5 At mobile home site, bear **R** and continue to port • Cross road to turn **L** along bank between municipal campsite and Plage de la Manchette • At its end bear **R** along road passing access to pretty Plage de la Pissotte • From here follow coastal path between houses and gardens, eventually emerging at road • Turn **R** down to Port de la Houle Causseul • *CA* downhill here, then branch **L** on balcony path **(beautiful view of the Plage de Rougeret below and the Hébihen archipelago out to sea)** • At ▣ turn **R** on road • Follow out to Pointe du Chevet – and maybe even continue to the island!

ÎLE DES HÉBIHENS

At low tide it is possible to walk out from the Pointe to the main island, passing the rocks of La Loge on the way. Excavations on Hébihens have proved the existence of a Gallo-Roman village, and found evidence of an 'industry' producing blocks of salt from seawater. Nowadays the only buildings of note are a defensive tower, built on its highest point in 1697, and a chapel dating from about the same time. Visitors to the island should not miss the panoramic view of the bay from its northern point – and then maybe take a brief turn on the beautiful beach, a wide crescent of golden sand, clearly visible from the Pointe du Chevet.

ST-JACUT-DE-LA-MER

On a long rocky finger crooked towards the île des Hébihens, St-Jacut is less of a resort than most of the north coast towns. Despite having several attractive beaches of fine white sand, it lacks that other necessary holiday ingredient, sea. In this shallow bay the sea retreats beyond the île des Hebihens and only at the height of the tide reaches the beaches of St-Jacut. Nevertheless, it is the peculiarities of this bay that favour the town's two main industries, mussel culture and oyster-farming. The rocky island of La Grande Roche separates the two – to the west, in the Bay of St-Cast, are the thick black buchots of mussels; to the east, as far as the causeway to Hébihens, are the oyster beds. Visitors to St-Jacut can also enjoy a variety of other shellfish found in abundance along its shores and it its rockpools.

10/1 From P at Pointe du Chevet, follow exit road 200m to take signed path on R • **For the next 2km you are following the most magnificent of coastal paths, skirting fine villas, climbing and ducking under the pine trees, and enjoying splendid views across the bay with its serried ranks of mussel posts**

10/2 Eventually, path runs along top of concrete seawall above beach, then climbs steps to grassy clifftop beside small P • Cross grassy space to path between high hedges descending to beach • Continue on beach, around headland to next sandy expanse - Plage du Ruet • Cross this beach to its access road (**At high tide it is not possible to get round headland. Instead continue on D62 to roundabout, follow Plage du Ruet access road R**) • Beside circular stone building, turn R on path • **The first field on the left contains a private chapel and a fine well built in 1802** • Continue over headland clothed in mixed woodland, then descend to wild empty sweep of Plage du Vauvert • Continue along dunes behind beach, then bear L, following edge of field all the way to path junction

Plage de Vauvert

10/3 Turn **L** (ignore waymarks) then immediately **R** on path down into valley • **Ahead are the impressive ruins of Château du Guildo** • Follow path climbing past château to reach road beside 🅿 • Turn **R** on road, follow down to D786 • Turn **R**, follow (with care) across bridge over mouth of Arguenon • Turn immediately **R** down steps to

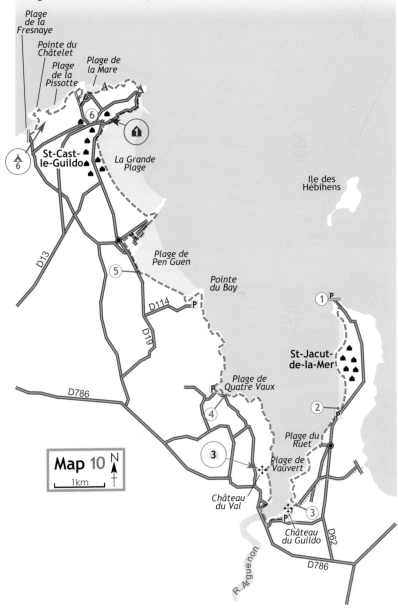

Plage de la Fresnaye

Pointe du Châtelet

Plage de la Pissotte

Plage de la Mare

St-Cast-le-Guildo

La Grande Plage

Ile des Hébihens

D13

Plage de Pen Guen

Pointe du Bay

D114

D19

D786

Plage de Quatre Vaux

St-Jacut-de-la-Mer

Map 10 N

1km

Plage du Ruet

Plage de Vauvert

Château du Val

Château du Guildo

D62

D786

R. Arguenon

CHÂTEAU DU GUILDO (CHÂTEAU DE GILLES DE BRETAGNE)

The château originates from the 12th century, but its alternative name refers to the short spell in the 1440s when it was owned by Gilles de Bretagne. Gilles was a gentle man for his time, a poet with many friends and a reputation for self-indulgence. His association with the British provoked the wrath of his brother Duc Francois I, who had him arrested. The château was later ransacked and Gilles remained in prison for three years before being assassinated.

The château had many more owners and was in the forefront of many more conflicts before being abandoned in the 17th century. It is currently being restored and a series of information boards have been set out to tell its story.

port • Leave port by access road • Immediately bear **R** between houses • Follow for 2km recently upgraded coastal path, rambling energetically through woods on steep banks of estuary, first skirting grounds of Château du Val

LES PIERRES SONNANTES (The Ringing Stones)

Take a few moments to divert along the shore of the estuary and you will come to some large smooth boulders. They are made of a hard stone known as amphibole (a bisilicate of calcium and magnesium), and if struck with a similar pebble will emit a strange metallic ringing sound. A romantic explanation for these stones relates to the hungry giant Gargantua, who apparently devoured all the catch of a fishing boat returning up the estuary. Unfortunately he ate the ballast too – and vomited it here on the bank.

Plage de Quatre Vaux

Amphibious mussel boats

10/4 At road follow **R** to beach and harbour of Quatre-Vaux • Walk down to back of beach, turn **L** up access road, then **R** across **P** (**The curious amphibious vehicles that are stored here are used to tend the mussel beds**) • Cross wooden footbridge to climb again through woodland • **CA** 2kms • **This splendid path, high above the sea, has fine views over the buchots of mussels in the bay** • After rounding Pointe du Bay (just below large **P**) path drops abruptly to follow dunes behind long sandy Plage de Pen Guen

10/5 Join main road at end of beach and walk uphill to first roundabout, turn **R** • 300m turn **R** on Rue des Peupliers • Almost at bottom of road, go **L** on broad earthen track • Bear **R** on road to reach

Plage de Pen Guen

51

Notre-Dame de la Garde

Pointe de la Garde • **The 3m high granite statue of Notre-Dame was erected here in 1945)** • Cross in front of statue, take rough track heading inland • Leave this via steps on **R** descending to Plage des Mielles **(also called the Grande Plage, one of St-Cast's many fine beaches)** • Walk along promenade (or along Plage des Mielles) • At end **CA** up road

10/6 At cross-roads, turn **R** on Rue du Port and keep ahead past unattractive modern buildings of port area • Continue up road ahead,

---

ST-CAST-LE-GUILDO

St-Cast's transition from fishing village to fashionable holiday resort began at the end of the 19th century and has continued ever since. Now scallops (Coquilles St-Jacques) and clams (palourdes) are the main catch, and shops and holiday apartments have been allowed to take over the port area. That said, nothing could detract from the scenic beauty of St-Cast's position. Around the peninsula are (at least) seven fine beaches, separated by high promontories of wild moorland.

The much-vaunted Battle of St-Cast took place in 1758, the time of the Seven Years War. British troops were besieging St-Malo when a storm forced their ships to take shelter off St-Cast. The men were obliged to make their way to St-Cast on foot, pillaging and burning as they went. On the Plage des Mielles they were finally trapped by French forces and vanquished in a bloody battle. In the Rue du Colonne (just behind the Grande Plage) the battle is commemorated by a column on which a French greyhound stands proud over an English leopard.

Plage des Mielles (La Grande Plage)

then leave it up steps on **R**, leading to curious monument (**Just a little farther up the road, a toposcope has been sited in front of the signalling station – it might be worth a diversion**)

MONUMENT DES ÉVADÉS
(Monument to the Escapees)

This double column commemorates brave French airmen who lost their lives in attempting to escape by boat to Britain, where they could join the Free French Forces –men who preferred 'to die standing rather than to live on their knees'.

The nearby cannon is a relic from the Battle of St-Cast (see p.52), lifted from the cliff below in 1990.

• From monument, bear **L** on path heading across moorland on clifftop

Just within sight of Plage de la Mare, a tall prow on the headland bears witness to the tragic story of the frigate Laplace. On 16th September 1950, this weather ship, heading for St-Malo, decided to anchor in the Bay of Fresnaye to ride out a storm. In the early hours of the morning, a mine remaining from the Second World War exploded under the ship, leaving 51 dead.

• Continue down beside camp site to Plage de la Mare • Take road ahead uphill • Turn **R**, then **R** again to follow round headland • **CA** with bird's eye views of little Plage de la Pissotte, before rounding Pointe du Châtelet and descending to Plage de la Fresnaye

Plage de la Mare

3. PRACTICAL INFORMATION

SHOPS & SERVICES
- **Dinard** TO 02 99 46 94 12 www.ot-dinard.com Mkt Tue, Thur, Sat
- **St-Lunaire** TO 02 99 46 31 09 www.saint-lunaire.com
- **St-Briac** TO 02 99 88 34 47 www.tourisme-saint-briac.fr
- **Lancieux** TO 02 96 86 25 37 www.lancieux-tourisme.fr
  Mkt Tues (seasonal)
- **St-Jacut-de-la-Mer** TO 02 96 27 71 91 www.saintjacutdelamer.com
  Mkt Fri
- **St-Cast-le-Guildo** TO 02 96 41 81 53 www.saintcastleguildo.fr Mkt Fri

ACCOMMODATION
Rand'Hôtel (geared to the needs of ramblers)
1. Rand'Hotel Port-Jacquet (on route) 32 Rue du Port, 22380
   St-Cast-le-Guildo 02 96 41 97 18 www.port-jacquet.com

Chambres d'Hôte
2. Mme Gaucher (200m) 35 rue de la Grève, 35800 St-Lunaire
   02 99 46 03 82 www.la-pensee.fr
3. Chateau du Val d'Arguénon (on route) N.D. du Guildo, 22380 St Cast le
   Guildo 02 96 41 07 03 www.chateauduval.com

Camping (nearest to route)
4. Camping Municipal le Port Blanc (on route) Rue de Sergeant Boulanger,
   35800 Dinard 02 99 46 10 74 Open April - Sept incl.
5. Camping Municipal les Mielles (250m) Rue Jules Jeunet, 22770
   Lancieux 02 96 86 22 98 Open April - Sept incl.
6. Camping Le Châtelet (200m) Rue des Nouettes, 22380
   St-Cast-le-Guildo 02 96 41 96 33 Open May to mid-Sept

TRANSPORT
Bus services: St-Malo – Dinard – Lancieux – St-Jacut-de-la-Mer
   – St-Cast-le-Guildo (Route 14) www.tibus.fr

Taxi: Allo Colas Taxis 02 99 46 73 07 Dinard
   Denis Deplanques 06 08 94 94 62 Saint-Briac-sur-Mer
   Allo Taxi 02 96 86 26 33 Lancieux
   Taxi Lecoq 02 96 27 71 08 St-Jacut

OTHER WALKS: (Dinard TO offer a map entitled *Balades à Dinard et sur la Côte d'Émeraude*)

- It is possible to follow the banks of the Frémur on either side as far as the tide mill of Rochegoude. For a 11km circuit follow signed route (yellow waymarks) from the mill to le Tertre Corieu (9/2 - 9/3), then coastal path to Lancieux and cut across headland to estuary.

- The narrow peninsula of St-Jacut lends itself to a circular walk (10km). Follow coastal path down west side as far as Point 10/3. Turn L to reach road, follow across peninsula (crossing D62) to the D26 on east side. Turn R a few paces to Point 9/4, continue L up east coast.

- The Tourist Office at St-Cast offers leaflets describing interesting short circular walks on the peninsula. (French text but good maps and routes well-waymarked).

4. St-Cast - Dahouët

Le Côte d'Émeraude 2

60 kms

Having left behind the urbanisation of St-Cast, the path now changes character, skirting high cliffs as it heads out towards Cap Fréhel. For the most part the cliffs are covered in woodland and in recent years much work has been done in creating paths passing through it, rather than taking the walker inland along roads as previously. It all makes a most pleasant if somewhat challenging ramble, with variation provided by little coves and fishing ports.

After leaving the wild landscapes of Cap Fréhel, the path visits in quick succession three of the most important resorts on the north Brittany coast – Sables-d'Or-les-Pins, Erquy and Val-André. This is not a stretch on which to forget your bathing costume! Between the resorts the route skirts many lesser-known beaches but there are also one or two sections of cliffside path where wild flowers and butterflies are found in abundance. Most glorious of all is the Cap d'Erquy, a designated conservation area where the colours of gorse and heather blend perfectly with the dark green pines and emerald sea far below. Although this is largely undemanding walking, the 'sting in the tail' is a couple of short but very sharp ascents just before the Pointe de Pléneuf.

Moulin de la Mer

DIRECTIONS

11/1 Cross road diagonally **R** to continue on coastal path to next beach, Plage de la Fosse • Cross beach access and **CA** up cliff on opposite side • At Port St-Jean, cross entrant stream, then road, **CA** through woodland • Follow path bending inland alongside estuary • At ruins of old mill turn **R** across front of mill, then **R** again to return on other side of estuary

Known as the **MOULIN DE LA MER**, in reality this mill had nothing to do with the sea. It was built around the end of the 17th century as a watermill to serve the villagers of St-Germain in grinding their corn. The old millstones can be seen at the back of the building.

• Continue along estuary 'beach' and leave it by steps to **L** of tide mill

Tide mill

At the mouth of the estuary, the old tide mill has been converted to a desirable residence. A dyke once crossed the mouth of the estuary, thus holding back the water at high tide, and providing power for the mill. It was destroyed in 2004.

• Keep **L** up rough service road • Almost at top, take path on **R** alongside fields, **CA** to Pointe St-Efficace • **The picnic tables here have a fine view of Fort de la Latte across the bay** • **CA** on path alongside hedge, then down through woodland beside bay, passing restored fontaine below village of St-Germain • Emerging through gap into open field, follow path sharp **L** alongside hedge to reach hamlet of la Fontaine Gourien • At road go **R**, then **R** again to walk down to D786 • Turn **R** along D786 • At bottom of hill bear **L** on grassy track to right of closed-down hotel • At farm buildings **CA** to road, turn **R** • 160m turn **R** again • Follow to D786

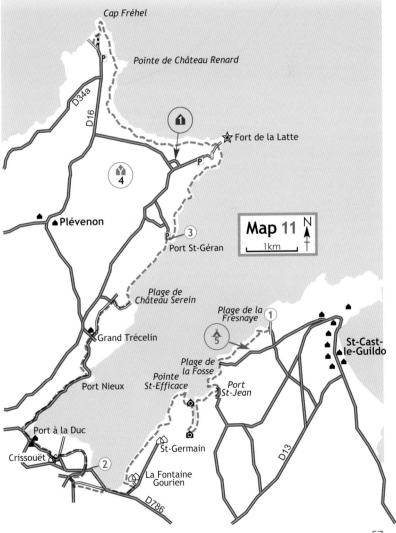

Port à la Duc

11/2 Cross to take road opposite, **CA** on track • Follow to hamlet of Crissouët • Bear **L** on road, then **R** and **R** again • Follow road down to fishing premises at Port à la Duc • Bear **R** on D786 over mouth of R. Frémur (walk through picnic area to avoid traffic) • On far side of bridge, turn **R** on road • Follow 1.6kms to small harbour of Port Nieux

Now silted up, Port Nieux was until the mid 19th century an important harbour exporting local grain.

• **CA** on road to Grand Trécelin • At cross-roads go **ahead** • **CA** on track into woodland • At road **CA** then double back **R** on broad track down to Plage de Château Serein • Turn **L** on beach and very soon turn **L** again up log steps • Follow path bending **R** beside wall • **CA** through woodland to tiny cove of Port St-Géran • **A flotilla of small boats is moored between the cliffs and the banks of mussels in the bay.**

Port St-Géran

FORT LA LATTE

This most sensationally positioned of forts has not surprisingly found its way into several films, most notably The Vikings in 1957. Although originally built by the Goyon-Matignon family in the 14th century, it owes its present appearance almost entirely to Louis XIV and Vauban. With steep cliffs guarding it on the seaward side and two drawbridges protecting it from the land, its keep has remained impregnable over the centuries. Guided tours (every day in summer, weekends only in winter) include the Guardroom, the cannonball foundry and the keep.

11/3 Cross **P** uphill to continue on obvious path • **All civilisation is now left behind as you continue for maybe an hour on the glorious coastal path to Fort La Latte** • Path crosses access road to fort

• **DIVERSION**: turn **L** here to **P** with toilets and summertime snack bar (crêperie 1km farther up road) **On the way you will pass a curious spindly menhir known as the Doigt de Gargantua (Gargantua's Finger).** Return same way to fort and coastal path

• **CA** from the fort on coastal path, now bordering cliffs in spectacular fashion all the

Le Doigt de Gargantua

Cap Fréhel

ESPACE EN RESTAURATION
Merci de rester sur les sentiers

way to Cap Fréhel (4km) • Passing
first through woodland, it soon
comes out on open moorland of low-growing gorse and heather. For
ecological reasons, it is requested that you stay strictly on the
path

Cap Fréhel has many visitors and its precipitous
cliffs and rough paths have been the scene of many
accidents. The authorities have recently installed a
series of coloured numbered posts to help identify
location in any emergency call.

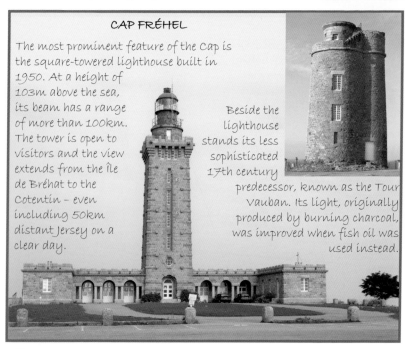

CAP FRÉHEL

The most prominent feature of the Cap is
the square-towered lighthouse built in
1950. At a height of
103m above the sea,
its beam has a range
of more than 100km.
The tower is open to
visitors and the view
extends from the Île
de Bréhat to the
Cotentin – even
including 50km
distant Jersey on a
clear day.

Beside the
lighthouse
stands its less
sophisticated
17th century
predecessor, known as the Tour
Vauban. Its light, originally
produced by burning charcoal,
was improved when fish oil was
used instead.

The cliffs around Cap Fréhel and the offshore rocky islands form a designated ornithological reserve. After passing the Pointe de Château Renard, gulls, guillemots, cormorants, oyster-catchers and a lot more can be seen on the cliffs known as La Fauconnière.

Beyond the lighthouses, paths lead out to the point itself where the jagged red cliffs with their towering stacks provide the drama. The two biggest stacks (Grande Fauconnière and Petite Fauconnière) are the favoured nesting place of a multitude of seabirds, although a whole 6km of this wild coastline has been declared an ornithological reserve. The simple restaurant, also called La Fauconnière, offers one of the best views of the site.

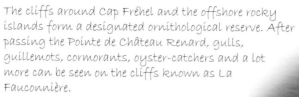

Stacks

12/1 Leave Cap Fréhel from western side of lighthouse • Follow coastal path snaking through heather along clifftop • After 1km path briefly touches road, then dives back into moorland before meeting road again • From here walk downhill beside road 700m

12/2 Just after turning to Plévenon, turn sharp **R** onto path behind hedge • Follow above beautiful beach (Les Grèves d'En Bas) and into pine woods to cross lower end of large campsite • Bear **R** through wooden barrier and continue on wide fenced track through dunes • At end of track branch **L** up steps to P • **Fine beach here, the Anse du Croc – the whole area is known as Pléherel-Plage**

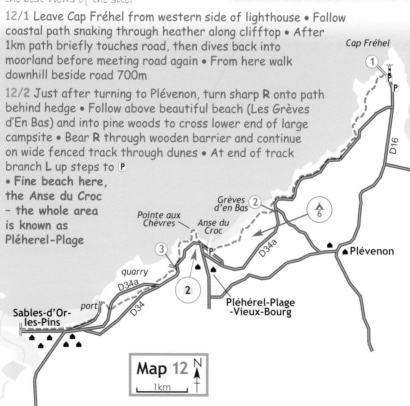

Anse du Croc

• Leave  🅿 by steep access road • At top, turn **R** on path out to Pointe aux Chèvres • **CA** before returning to the main road (D34A) • Follow alongside road, around bend

12/3 At quarry entrance, take path up into woodland on **R** • Follow 500m to road • Cross road and **CA** through pine plantations • At road, go **L** 20m, then cross to path • Rounding shoulder of hill, path soon descends steeply to track above beach • **On the right is a small commercial port used for the export of stone from the quarries** • Turn **L** along track to road • **CA** along promenade above golden beach • Follow promenade to very end

SABLES-D'OR-LES-PINS

Sables d'Or les-Pins began life as a commercial enterprise, the dream of one Roland Brouard. At the beginning of the 20th century, with rail travel increasing and sea-bathing gaining popularity, he imported golden sand to the site and built fine residences and hotels to attract the wealthy from the cities. Casinos, golf courses and tennis courts were added to the scene. Eventually the stock market crash of 1929 put an end to it all, and Brouard died penniless, a few years later. After the war years regeneration began and today les Sables is again a well-serviced though not yet high-profile resort.

13/1 At end of promenade drop down to **L**, curving back and continuing under pines • **Here you are alongside a marais (salt marsh), the tidal estuary of the River Islet. Egrets and curlews may be seen wandering through the thick carpet of salt-loving vegetation.**

Estuary of the River Islet

• At D34
turn **R**, still
alongside marais
• At its far end fork
R • 500m at **L** bend, go **ahead** on track across two old railway bridges

The bridges once carried the narrow gauge track of the Petit Train des Côtes-du-Nord (see p.82). The line closed in 1949.

• After second bridge, go down steps on **R** to track alongside reclaimed polder • Continue on tarmac road • At T-junction go **L** (**R crosses the marais on a sandy track**) and climb (**good views across the bay to the Pointe du Champ du Port**) ignoring waymarks on left • At **TJ** turn **R** and descend to camp site at the point • Go under barrier to **R** of camp entrance • Continue on sandy track to next beach (Plage St-Michel) with its offshore island

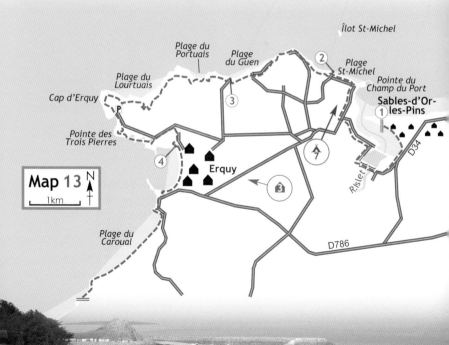

Îlot St-Michel

Plage du Portuais

Plage du Guen

Plage St-Michel

Pointe du Champ du Port

Plage du Lourtuais

Cap d'Erquy

P

Sables-d'Or-les-Pins

① ②

③

Pointe des Trois Pierres

④

Erquy

⑦

R. Islet

D34

Map 13 N

1km

③

Plage du Caroual

D786

Pointe du Champ du Port

63

Legend has it that there was merely a promontory here when the archangel Michael arrived pursued by the Devil. The Archangel stamped his foot, the rocky causeway collapsed leaving an island, and the Devil fell into the sea. Since the 13th century the island has been a sacred place dedicated to St-Michael (St-Michel) and at one time Cistercian monks celebrated mass here every year on St-Michael's Day. The current chapel dates from the end of the 18th century, and it is possible to reach it on foot at low tide.

13/2 From beach go up access road past little crêperie, then turn R on Impasse de Doue de Lormet, going uphill behind holiday homes • At far end, turn R to descend by road to Plage de Fosse Eyrand • At seafront, follow road L towards Holiday Centre

The cliffs here have been quarried and huge blocks of stone divide the road from the pebble beach. This rock is the pink sandstone (grès rose) for which Erquy is famous. A crystalline sediment from some 480 million years ago, it is the 'cement' of silicon tinged with iron that produces its characteristic colour. (See p.71)

Pink sandstone

• Beyond the Holiday Centre, follow short section of coastal path to road through new housing development • At its end, turn L on road heading inland and cross wooden bridge on R • Climb cliff before descending to Plage du Guen

13/3 Walk up beach access road, turn R on path climbing to moorland • Follow in and out of valleys, descend to Plage du Portuais • Climb again above Plage de Lourtuais • CA to Cap d'Erquy a headland of gorse, heather and pine trees. From the tip there are views westward as far as the Pointe de l'Arcouest and the Île de Bréhat • Follow path left to P • CA on road 300m, then take signed path on R leading to Pointe des Trois Pierres

The building just ahead as you turn was once a guard-room and powder store. Farther along at the point, the similar building was a much more sinister Four à Boulets. Built in 1794, its purpose was to raise cannon balls to 'red heat' before firing, in order to set ablaze the wooden ships of the English fleet.

Erquy harbour and town beyond

- Beyond Four à Boulets, follow precarious path clinging to the cliff above fish market and harbour

The lakes passed here are known as 'Les Lacs Bleus' – even though the water is distinctly brown. They were created as a result of 19th century quarrying for stone that was used to build the pavements of Paris.

- At road, turn **R** • 400m (just before Erquy sign), turn **R** down steps to road • Continue down and turn **R** again down steps to reach seafront near harbour

---

ERQUY

Unlike its neighbours on either side, Erquy is an old town, and was thriving as a fishing port long before it became a resort. It is traditionally famed for its scallops – Coquilles St-Jacques – and these are still an important catch in the winter months. At other times there are sole, turbot and other coastal fish. The present day fleet numbers about 80 boats. Erquy's development as a resort came with the arrival of the railway at the beginning of the 20th century. Today it claims ten beaches – certainly the coastal path here passes them all so you can work it out for yourself.

Not surprisingly the town has its place in the rich fund of Breton legends. The story goes that somewhere offshore there is a drowned city – some say this is the Breton capital of Ys, swamped when its princess opened the forbidden sea gates, others claim it to be Nazado, a city of corruption, cursed by the giant Gargantua.

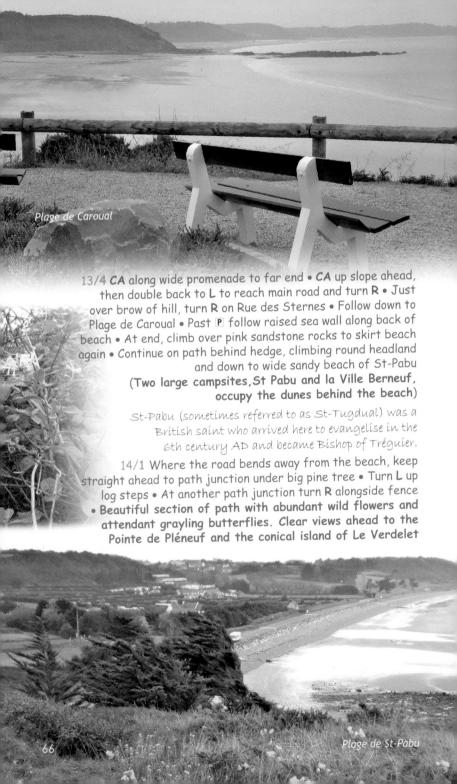

Plage de Caroual

13/4 **CA** along wide promenade to far end • **CA** up slope ahead, then double back to **L** to reach main road and turn **R** • Just over brow of hill, turn **R** on Rue des Sternes • Follow down to Plage de Caroual • Past ℗ follow raised sea wall along back of beach • At end, climb over pink sandstone rocks to skirt beach again • Continue on path behind hedge, climbing round headland and down to wide sandy beach of St-Pabu

(Two large campsites, St Pabu and la Ville Berneuf, occupy the dunes behind the beach)

St-Pabu (sometimes referred to as St-Tugdual) was a British saint who arrived here to evangelise in the 6th century AD and became Bishop of Tréguier.

14/1 Where the road bends away from the beach, keep straight ahead to path junction under big pine tree • Turn **L** up log steps • At another path junction turn **R** alongside fence • **Beautiful section of path with abundant wild flowers and attendant grayling butterflies. Clear views ahead to the Pointe de Pléneuf and the conical island of Le Verdelet**

Plage de St-Pabu

Le Verdelet

• Go down to back of beach and follow clear signs to continue along bank of pebbles behind beach of Nantois • At end of bank follow path bending away and climb very steeply to clifftop • Descend to 🅿 on far side • **The walk from here, Plage des Vallées, to the Pointe de Pléneuf is very popular with the local population, despite its energetic beginning**

14/2 Cross 🅿 to go up steps opposite • Climb long series of log steps leading to clifftop • Continue along cliffside beneath handsome residences (**a picturesque approach to the Pointe de Pléneuf**)

A viewing area with bench looks out over Le Verdelet, an ornithological reserve, home to gulls, terns and cormorants among others. The island can be reached by a causeway at low tide.

• **CA** round headland • Take steps on **R** leading down to harbour • From harbour **CA** - **EITHER** on beach **OR** along pedestrianised promenade around bay

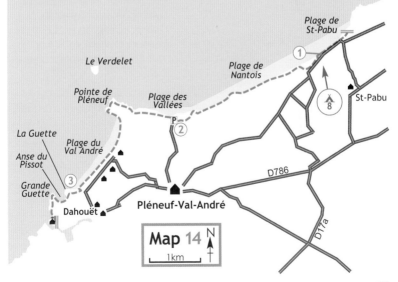

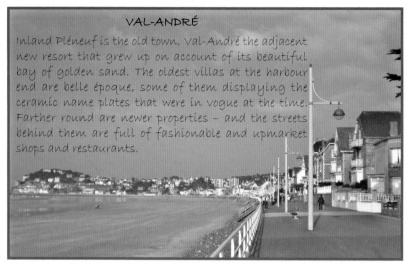

VAL-ANDRÉ

Inland Pléneuf is the old town, Val-André the adjacent new resort that grew up on account of its beautiful bay of golden sand. The oldest villas at the harbour end are belle époque, some of them displaying the ceramic name plates that were in vogue at the time. Farther round are newer properties – and the streets behind them are full of fashionable and upmarket shops and restaurants.

14/3 Just before end of promenade, take narrow road L, then bear R up passageway between walls • At top turn R on road to descend to coastal path

In doing this you have bypassed the headland of la Guette. The blockhaus on the headland formed an important part of Rommel's 'Atlantic Wall' – and Rommel himself stayed at the Villa Cornu at the north end of the promenade when he came to inspect it.

Dahouët

• Follow coastal path around Anse du Pissot and climb to headland of Grande Guette (where an old Corps de Guard dating from 1750 has been restored) • CA past this to descend to harbour at Dahouët

At the entrance to the harbour stands an oratory dedicated to Notre Dame de la Garde. It was built to seek the protection of the Virgin for ships setting out on long fishing expeditions to distant waters, and to commemorate those who did not return. The original cast iron statue was replaced by one of more durable granite in 1964.

4. PRACTICAL INFORMATION

SHOPS & SERVICES (After St-Cast there are no services near the route before Fort La Latte)
- **St-Cast-le-Guildo** TO 02 96 41 81 53 www.saintcastleguildo.fr Mkt Fri
- **Cap Fréhel / Sables-d'Or-les-Pins** TO 02 96 41 53 81
  www.pays-de-frehel.com
- **Erquy** TO 02 96 72 30 12 www.erquy-tourisme.com Mkt Fri
- **Pléneuf-Val-André** TO 02 96 72 20 55 www.val-andre.org
  Mkt Tue (seasonal)
- **Pléherel-Plage**   • **Dahouët**

ACCOMMODATION

Hotels
1. Hotel Ushuaia (1km from Fort la Latte) La Pointe du Fort la Latte, 22240 Fréhel 02 96 41 41 61

Chambres d'Hôte
2. Mme Garnier (300m) rue Bellevue 22240 Pléhérel Plage 02 96 41 46 18
   augrandbanc@wanadoo.fr

Gîte de Séjour
3. Les Bruyères (1.5km) les Ruaux, Rue des Hôpitaux, 22430 Erquy
   02 96 72 31 59

Auberge de Jeunesse (Youth Hostel)
4. Auberge de Jeunesse de Cap Fréhel (1.5km from Port St-Géran) Ville Hardrieux, 22240 Plévenon 02 96 41 48 98 64 beds Open April - Sept

Camping
5. Camping La Fontaine (on route) La Ville Norme, 22380 St-Cast-le-Guildo 02 96 41 95 64 Open late March to late October
6. Camping le Pont de l'Étang (on route) Pléherel-Plage, 22240 Fréhel 02 96 41 40 45 Open April - Sept
7. Camping des Hautes Grées (on route) rue St-Michel, 22430 Erquy 02 96 72 34 78 www.camping-hautesgrees.com Open mid-March - Sept
8. Camping la Ville Berneuf (on route) Plage Ville Berneuf, 22370 Pléneuf-Val-André 02 96 72 28 20
   www.camping-plagevilleberneuf.com Open mid-March - early Nov

TRANSPORT

Bus services: Cap Fréhel (Plévenon) - Plurien – Erquy – Pléneuf - St-Brieuc Tibus Route 2 0810 22 22 22 www.tibus.fr

Taxi: Taxis Castins 02 96 41 86 16 St-Cast-le-Guildo
        Taxis du Cap 02 96 72 32 32 Erquy

OTHER WALKS

Tracks and minor roads can be used to complete circuits including Cap Fréhel and Pointe de la Latte.

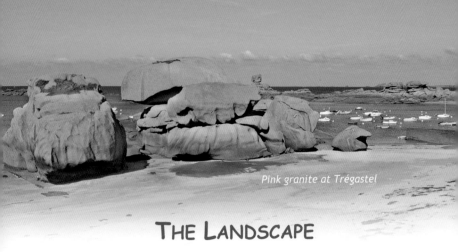

Pink granite at Trégastel

THE LANDSCAPE

Brittany, it is said, has a heart of stone – and certainly the whole region is built on the Armorican Massif, granite that was formed in the Primary Era and is some of the oldest rock in the world. But this north coast is different and in places it almost seems that someone has taken a paintbrush along to give it brighter tones. The gnarled curious shapes of deep red rock that form the Pink Granite Coast are its most amazing feature, but the pink sandstone of Erquy and Cap Frehel is also quite distinctive and farther west at Primel and le Diben the rock has a strange orange glow in the evening light. And all this rocky spectacle is laid out along a coast that has so many dog-tooth indentations that its profile is quite bizarre. Why are there so many long river valleys reaching into the heart of the land, why so many long promontories, and why all the reefs and islands stretching out far into the sea? The whole looks as if it had been thrown from a distance by a giant hand.

Celtic Brittany is not short of mythological explanations for its unusual features. But the story begins some 600 million years ago, when all France was under water. At this time the upheaval known as the Hercynian Fold pushed many of the mountains of France out of the sea, among them the Armorican Massif that now includes all Brittany and part of Normandy. The mountains of Brittany were then as high as the Alps, but erosion over the millennia following left only the low Monts d'Arrée and the Montaignes Noires of the interior. In the tertiary Era, about 60 million years ago, underground rocking movements caused the splits in Brittany's coastline. It was much later, when sea levels rose at the end of the Ice Age, that those long clefts were invaded by the sea. North Brittany's estuaries are technically rias, created by flooding from the sea, rather than by the rivers that flow into them. In the same period the lowest land around the coast was also flooded, and the mountains and hills became the islands and

Erquy's pink sandstone

reefs of today. Erosion of mountains that were farther inland has produced high cliffs like those at Cap Fréhel.

So much for the morphology of the landscape, but what about those colours? Travelling west, the first time you will probably be aware that the coastline is wearing a red tinge is on the approach to Cap Fréhel. Some of the stacks off the Cape display layers of colour ranging from orange to deep mauve. The cliffs are made of old red sandstone, maybe 400 million years old. The sandstone is composed of tiny grains of parent rock pressed tightly together over the millennia and cemented with silicate. It is the iron ore deposits in the silicate that turn the rock red. A little farther along, the same colour suffuses the sands of Sables d'Or les Pins, and both here and in Erquy the stone is quarried. Erquy's Pink Sandstone (Grès Rose) is renowned throughout France and much of it has found its way to the pavements of Paris. Walking along the shore near the quarries of Fosse-Eyrand you can see some of the cut stone and appreciate its delicate tints.

Round the corner and facing the Bay of St-Brieuc, the cliffs have an even brighter orange colour, but these cliffs are much younger, being composed of sediments laid down somewhere between 350,000 and 10,000 years ago. At

Sedimentary layers at l'Hôtellerie

The golden scorched colour near Castel Meur

l'Hôtellerie, the striations of the cliff correspond to different sediments laid down over that period, and to the change in sea levels.

West of St-Brieuc the coast is particularly ragged and rocky with tidal river valleys winding miles inland. The golden scorched colour is still present, particularly in the Île de Bréhat and its archipelago. But the best is yet to come. After Perros-Guirec the coast becomes another world, a surreal world of enormous deep red rocks, eccentrically shaped and improbably balanced, a stunning contrast to the calm turquoise sea. This is the Pink Granite Coast, and back at the cove of Pors Kamor, where the rocks are at their most bizarre, the Maison du Littoral attempts to give an explanation. Granite is igneous rock, and it seems that the vein of magma here is a mere 300 million years old as opposed to the 400 million-year-old rock on either side. After cooling in the depths and being pushed to the surface the vein appeared as concentric arcs of rock in which the particles were of different size. The coarsest grain was on the outside, next to the ancient granite, and it is this band that extends from Pors Rolland round to the Île Milliau at Trébeurden. Coarse grained granite is more easily eroded and the loosened particles have been washed into cracks, grinding at them to make them larger, and so creating the stacked appearance. The brilliant red colour again comes from the quantity of iron oxide. If you walk the Sentier des Douaniers between Perros-Guirec and Ploumanac'h you will see the difference between the natural dusky-red stone and the cut and polished version, which is used to number the formations. The latter is particularly beautiful, and has been used for headstones, sculptures and building façades.

5. Dahouët - St-Brieuc
Bay of St-Brieuc
36 kms

There are no resorts on this section, and no towns either. Instead there is wild moorland, and high cliffs towering over a shallow bay dominated by the black stakes of the mussel farmers. The one major break in the cliffs comes at the estuary of the Gouessant, where it is necessary to walk 2km inland to cross – and even here the banks of the river are precipitous. Beyond the Gouessant, a last headland guards the entrance to the Anse d'Yffiniac, the innermost part of the Bay of St-Brieuc. Here at last the coastal path leaves the heights and comes down to earth beside a dense marsh of saltworts, a designated natural reserve rich in wildlife. Beside its shore the track of a former narrow-gauge railway takes you on to St-Brieuc, with a final amble beside the commercial port.

DAHOUËT

Dahouët has long been a fishing port, and in 1509 its mariners were among the first to cross the Atlantic to fish off Newfoundland. Cod fishing off Iceland similarly became important and the fine old buildings on the quayside were the homes of some of the richest fishermen. Here also stands the old Customs House, and farther on, where the main road crosses at the head of the port, is a former tide mill. The newer pleasure port is known as the Port des Salines, a reminder of its location on the site of a rather unsuccessful venture into salt extraction.

DIRECTIONS (see map opposite)

15/1 Walk alongside harbour at Dahouët, then go **R** on road and **R** again • **CA** right round Port de Plaisance • In front of 'Val Plaisance' building, bear **L** up road and take first **R** • 100m turn **R** onto coastal path and **CA** (crossing ends of 2 small roads) to Port Morvan • Here cross beach access road and **CA** up Rue de la Fontenelle opposite • At top keep ahead, then branch **R** onto coastal path • Follow around field then along cliff

15/2 **CA** past **P** at Plage de Vauglin • Follow clifftop path 1.4km to la Cotentin • **Here there is a fine ceramic toposcope beside the path**

Toposcope

La Cotentin sits atop a particularly lofty cliff down which a steep track descends to the beach. If the tide is not high, it is worth going down to explore the caves on the left at the bottom of the slope.

Port Morvan

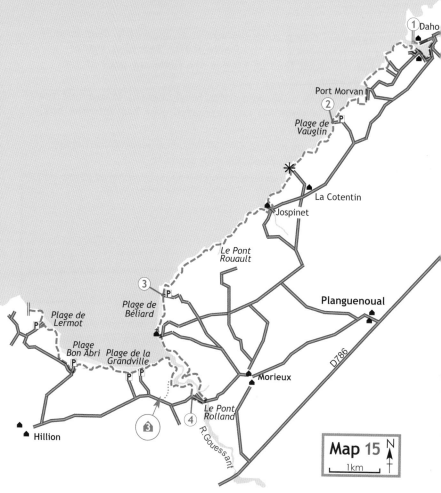

- **CA** on clifftop path to Jospinet • Here follow **L** and descend to road
- Turn **R** and **CA** over junction to cross bridge • 50m turn **R** onto coastal path and **CA**

The buildings of the harbour at Jospinet look a little run down, but this is still an important centre for mussel cultivation. Fresh shellfish can be bought from the big enterprise at the road junction, while the seafood restaurant (seasonal) on the harbourside enjoys an excellent reputation.

After Jospinet, only a quick dip into the valley at le Pont Rouault breaks the long walk over the lonely cliffs. The first sign of civilisation for more than an hour is the little car park at the Plage de Béliard.

At high tide this is a pleasant little family beach; at low tide the sea is not even in sight – it has retreated over 3km into the bay, the Anse de Morieux.

15/3 **CA** past Plage de Béliard • At St-Maurice descend past chapel to P behind beach and **CA** on coastal path opposite

ST-MAURICE

The chapel here dates from the 19th century, although it has recently undergone restoration after bombardment in the last World War. It is thought that there had been a previous chapel on the site for some 700 years.

• At mouth of River Gouessant follow inland to climb high along steep wooded sides of valley • Descend to cross stream and **CA** to road at Le Pont Rolland

DIVERSION: turn **L** and **CA** on road 1km to Morieux - **CA** 2kms further to dovecote at Planguenoual if desired - return to Le Pont Rolland

MORIEUX

The village of Morieux is well worth a visit. A recent restoration of the church revealed an amazing collection of frescoes dating from between the 12th and the 17th centuries. Scenes from the life of Christ, a Passion series, the Last Supper, a calendar of months and more had all been covered in whitewash for more than 200 years, but have now been reinstated in beautiful ochre tints.

Having made the diversion to Morieux it is a further 2kms to the outskirts of Planguenoual, to take a look at the splendid 16th century dovecote of Vaujoyeux with places for 1,000 birds. Having a unique 4-towered design, it has recently been the subject of painstaking restoration.

Pont Rolland hydro-electric station

MAIN ROUTE: turn **R** on road across river Gouessant • To the right are the buildings of the hydro-electric scheme, and to the left, the barrage constructed in 1935. Several water mills were drowned at the time.

15/4 Uphill 250m at **L** bend, take path into woodland on **R** • Follow along opposite bank of river • Pass a board announcing that you are overlooking the site of Crémur, a Gallo-Roman village and harbour • At path junction, Gîte d'Étape at La Grandville is signed 5 minutes away • **CA** on main path following bends of river • At coast there are views across rivermouth to Chapelle St-Maurice

Valley of the Gouessant

Plage de la Grandville

Just a few metres up the road at Grandville is the colourful house that was once the holiday home of Professor of Philosophy **Georges Palantes**. He had it built in 1907 and stayed there every summer until his suicide in August 1925.

• **CA**, skirting fields to two P︎s in quick succession at Plage de la Grandville • Beyond la Grandville, the path quickly reaches the dunes of Bon Abri • **This is an ecologically important protected area and the path first runs between wooden posts and wire fencing** • After fencing, go **R** at fork and **CA** past ponds to road at Plage Bon Abri • Turn **L** on road to junction (before complex of mussel cultivation sheds) and turn **R** (small open air café here, open in summer only)

Clearly in sight at low tide are the ranks of mussel stakes that stretch right across this bay. Mussel farming began here in the 1960s when cultivators from Charente were looking for new places to practise their trade. Ropes bearing young mussels are wound around the posts between May and August each year. The mussels are then allowed to grow on for about 18 months before being harvested. This particular area provides 10% of France's national production.

Pointe des Gouettes

- **CA** past campsite
- 350m turn **R** onto coastal path • At Plage de Lermot, go **L** up access road, then sharp **R** through P and small picnic area to **CA** on coastal path

16/1 **CA** to Pointe des Gouettes • Turn **R** to *table d'orientation* • **CA** on obvious path, across concrete steps down from P, to Pointe du Grouin • **The top of the old blockhaus here has been fenced to provide a viewing platform - St-Brieuc clearly visible across the bay** • **CA** along eastern shore of Anse d'Yffiniac to Grève de St-Guimont

The mudflats below are covered only at the height of the tide. At other times you may see shell-fishers out there (scallops and clams are abundant) or even horses being exercised. It almost looks as if you could cross directly to St-Brieuc - but beware! Those who frequent this bay know where the river has carved its channels, and understand how quickly the tide comes in. This is no place for the uninitiated!

- **CA** 800m to signed path leading up to Maison de la Baie **(DIVERSION: 100m - displays of local wildlife)**

Grève de St-Guimont

NATURE RESERVE OF THE BAY OF ST-BRIEUC

The Reserve, established in 1998, comprises the Anse de Morieux and the Anse d'Yffiniac. From the depths of these bays the sea retires more than 7km, leaving behind a vast area of sand and mudflats where life is governed by the rhythm of the tides. The Reserve is on the grand axis of bird migration from northern Europe to Africa and every year it welcomes some 50,000 avian visitors. Most spend the whole winter here, growing fat on the molluscs and crustaceans that live just under the sand. For a few others it is just a short-stay hotel and restaurant to enjoy before moving on. Conspicuous inhabitants at high tide are the flocks of Canada geese and ducks like mallard, shelduck and wigeon, while at low tide egrets, curlews, dunlins and other waders take over the scene.

Although the bird life here is very evident it is by no means the only important ingredient of the Reserve. The wealth of plants on the salt marsh, the orchids of the dunes and the frogs, lizards and grasssnakes of the inland lakes all have their own ecological significance.

Maison de la Baie

● **CA** on coastal path again, briefly touching road at l'Hôtellerie

The 'silt' cliffs here demonstrate cycles of climate change over the last half million years. The striations represent the associated variations in sea level.

● **DIVERSION:** to Hillion, 500m up road from L'Hôtellerie

The town of **HILLION** has two buildings of particular interest - the church of Saint-Jean-Baptiste with its original Romanesque nave, and the 16th century dovecote of Clos Guegan, where the lord of the manor once kept 600 birds.

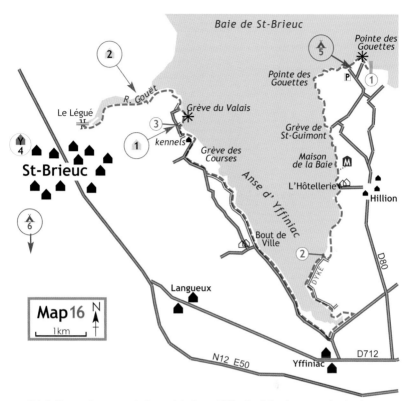

- **CA** 1.4kms above and alongside bay **(filled with dense salt-loving vegetation - the technical name is schorre – see p.46)**

16/2 Descend to **CA** along top of dyke, then beside it on broad rough track • Where track swings **L**, turn **R** and return to top of dyke • Follow path behind (and through) gardens to road • Turn **R** along narrow (sometimes busy) road to junction on outskirts of Yffiniac • Turn **R** and **CA** on road 2.5kms alongside vegetation-filled bay • At end, **CA** on track (bed of former railway line)

View from the dyke

CHEMINS DES CÔTES DU NORD

Construction work for this narrow gauge line began in 1852 and the last section of it was closed down just over a hundred years later. Today, at the place known as Bout de Ville (or Boutdeville), trains and rolling stock are being restored. If the sheds are open, the volunteers carrying out this work welcome visitors.

In close proximity to the railway, a museum built on the site of a former tile and brick-making factory (la Briqueterie) offers an insight into the way of life in this bay in former times.

• Follow pleasant track through woodland with good views across the Reserve • At road, turn **R**

Below you and to the right is the site of the **COURSE DES GRÈVES**, one of the oldest horse-racing courses in France. Opened under the direction of Napoleon I in 1807, the original course was merely a straight strip 2km in length (the horses had to turn round a post and come back again). Great crowds from St-Brieuc and beyond came to watch the fun.

The estuary is overlooked by the **TOUR CESSON**. This now crumbling octagonal tower was built on the site of a Roman castrum by Jean IV, Duke of Brittany, in 1395 to control and defend St-Brieuc. It was strategically important during the Wars of Religion (1589-1598) and was taken by the Comte de Brissac in 1598. At the request of the local population he ordered its dismantlement, during which half the tower collapsed. It was eventually decided to keep what remained as an aid to navigation.

ST-BRIEUC

The town sits on a plateau high above the sea and is cut through by the deep gorges of two rivers, the Gouët and the Gouédic. Bridges span them both and from the port of le Légué you can look up to the busy traffic on the N12, 70m above the canalised Gouët. The height is impressive, but the best way to access the town on foot is by a newly-restored footpath through the ornamental grounds of the Villa Rohannec'h on the south bank.

For the capital town of the Côtes d'Armor department, St-Brieuc has not a lot to offer its visitors other than a fine array of fashionable shops and a good twice weekly market. Nevertheless, anyone making the trip will find it worth taking a look at the 13th century cathedral, a solid building with a fortified appearance, and then straying off into the nearby streets where there are some fine half-timbered buildings.

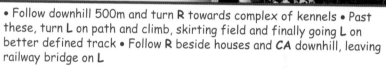

• Follow downhill 500m and turn **R** towards complex of kennels • Past these, turn **L** on path and climb, skirting field and finally going **L** on better defined track • Follow **R** beside houses and **CA** downhill, leaving railway bridge on **L**

16/3 In complex of small holiday chalets, take **R** turn (signed) down track between chalets • At end bear **L** to skirt more chalets on cliff edge • At viewing platform above beach (Grève du Valais) go down steps and **CA** on promenade • At end turn **L** up beach access road and take first **R** to double back on broad track between chalets • **CA** on narrow path along cliff edge • **CA** through woodland around headland • Follow **R** and down to cross railway beside quay • Turn **L** and follow quayside to Pont Tournant (Swing Bridge) • Cross to Port du Légué

Mouth of the R. Gouët

5. PRACTICAL INFORMATION

SHOPS & SERVICES

- **Morieux** (1 km off route) : bar/restaurant, food shops
- **Hillion** (500m off route) : all services
- **Yffiniac** (500m off route) : all services
- **St-Brieuc** TO 0 825 00 22 22 www.baiedesaintbrieuc.com

ACCOMMODATION

Chambres d'Hôte

1. Mme Dolédec (on route) 9 rue Cdt d'Estiennes d'Orves, 22000 St-Brieuc 02 96 61 75 53

2. Maison du Phare (on route 1km into next section) 93 rue de la Tour, Port du Légué, 22190 Plerin 02 96 33 34 65 www.maisonphare.com

Gite d'étape

3. Les Mouettes Rieuses (400m) Crémur, 22120 Hillion   06 72 39 08 27 Small dairy farm with accommodation for 15 people in rooms for 2/3 http://les.mouettes.rieuses.chez-alice.fr Open all year

Youth Hostel

4. Manoir de la Ville Guyomard (2.5kms) 'les villages', 22000 St-Brieuc 02 96 78 70 70 www.fuaj.org Open all year

Camping

5. Camping Bellevue Mer (200m) La Pointe des Gouettes, 22120 Hillion 02 96 32 20 39 www.bellevuemer.com Open April - September

6. Camping des Vallées (3.5kms) Parc de Brézillet, Bd. Paul Doumer, 22000 St-Brieuc 02 96 94 05 05 Open all year.

TRANSPORT

Bus services: Tibus Line 2 (Fréhel - St-Brieuc) stops at Dahouët, Morieux, La Grandville, Hillion and Yffiniac www.tibus.fr

Yffiniac is also served by TUB (Transports Urbains Briochins) buses. Line 14 goes to the bus station in St-Brieuc centre. From there, Line 6 stops near the Pont Tournant and Line 16 goes to Les Rosaires (see p.87) www.tubinfo.fr

Taxis Taxis Griffons 02 96 94 70 70 St-Brieuc

　　　'Allo' Taxis 02 96 01 95 47 St-Brieuc

OTHER WALKS

The headland of Hillion lends itself to both long and short circular walks. Two circuits here are described in a folder entitled *Balades en Baie de Saint-Brieuc* (in French only, but with excellent maps - can be purchased from TOs). The same folder will also provide you with a 9km circuit incorporating the west shore of the Anse d'Yffiniac, as well as several more routes farther up the coast.

In the same series, *Balades en Côtes de Penthièvre* describes a 10km circular walk linking Dahouët and Jospinet.

6. St-Brieuc - Bréhec

Goëlo

48 kms

This is truly a headland-hopping section, and although it starts in the depths of the gorge of the Gouët at St-Brieuc, it is not long before you reach the first promontory, the Pointe du Roselier. The toposcope here is just one of several on the route, and by the end of the day, familiarisation with the distant scene is guaranteed! In addition there are a couple of old Corps du Gardes (Coastguard posts) and even a rare Four à Boulets that once heated up cannon balls for firing at wooden ships. The many beaches are not all that well known but are very well cared for, and very popular with the local residents. At even the smallest of them there is usually a café open in summertime. The main resorts of Binic and St-Quay-Portrieux both have fine beaches, but also function as fishing ports where you may be fortunate enough to see the catch being brought home. The section ends with the highest cliffs in Brittany, and the little cove known as Plage Bonaparte that played its part in a most daring and successful wartime Resistance operation.

Pont tournant - swing bridge - Port du Légué

DIRECTIONS:

17/1 Having crossed Pont Tournant, turn **R** alongside road • **CA** 2kms • At **L** bend climbing inland turn **R** on tarmac path between houses • At end, turn **L** on Rue des Trois Pierres • At **TJ**, turn **R** down to beach at St-Laurent-de-la-Mer • **CA** along promenade • At end turn **L**, **R**, then **L** again to climb past Centre Helio-Marin • Here turn **R** on coastal path behind buildings • **CA** 500m join road • Follow 250m then bear **R** on coast path • **CA** to Pointe du Roselier

POINTE DU ROSELIER The path comes up beside the restored four à boulets, poised on the cliff to deliver red-hot cannon balls to the English fleet! Beside the car park, a small hedged area contains both a mariners' memorial and a fine table d'orientation.

• Cross **P** and **CA** on coastal path, soon descending to Martin Plage

R. Gouët

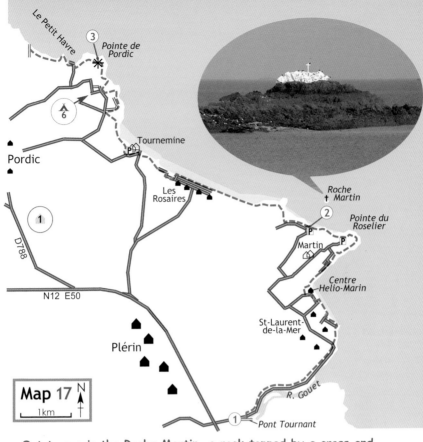

Map 17

N

1km

• Out to sea is the Roche Martin, a rock topped by a cross and painted white as a marker for boats. A sand bar connects it to the beach.

17/2 **Erosion of the cliff has necessitated a deviation here** • Walk up beach access road 500m • Almost at top turn **R** on track that returns to old coastal path • Follow **L** and down to track behind pebble beach • At end **CA** on promenade at Les Rosaires • Take last road **L** from promenade • At **TJ** turn **R** • 150m **R** again downhill to bear **L** on 'balcony' road parallel to and above beach • At end **CA** on coastal path into woodland • Descend to beach access road in Tournemine • Turn **R**, then immediately **L** on road

Les Rosaires

Le Petit Havre

inland • Past 🅿 turn **R** onto coast path, climbing again • 600m follow inland along field edge to road • Turn sharp **R** here • Follow rough road 700m, looping downhill (**almost overhanging the cliff at one point - this is both a viewpoint and a hang-gliding site. Just don't get too near the edge!**) and **CA** back to road • At junction bear **R**, then bear **R** again on track following cliff-top around Pointe de Pordic

17/3 **On L, log steps lead up to artistic toposcope beside tidied-up ruins of old Corps de Garde** • **CA** on cliff-top path and down to Le Petit Havre • **Here a Sentier de Découverte (Discovery Trail) points out some of the natural features of the area** • Go **R** downhill, then **L** onto coastal path

BINIC

In previous times Binic was the premier cod fishing port in France, its seafaring inhabitants making frequent excursions to the waters off Newfoundland and Iceland. Today the fishing fleet is much reduced in size, and instead around 500 pleasure craft are accommodated in the basin, with a couple of hundred more beyond the lock gate. The town has become an attractive holiday venue, with good family beaches and lively bars and restaurants along the colourful quayside.

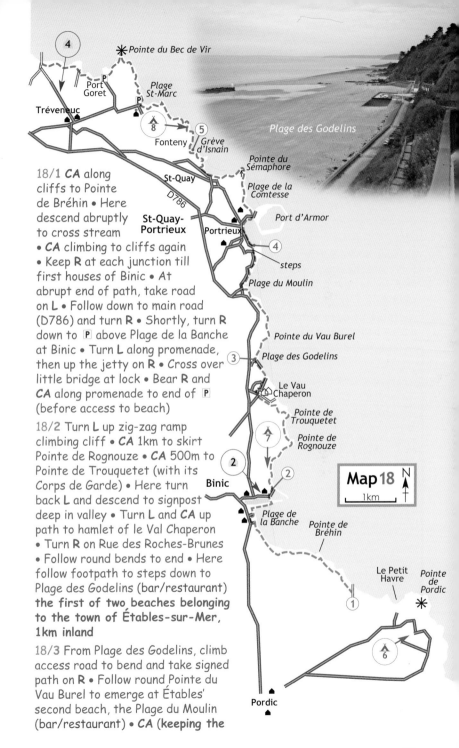

※ *Pointe du Bec de Vir*

④

P
Port
Goret

P

Plage
St-Marc

Tréveneuc

⑧

⑤

Fonteny

Grève
d'Isnain

St-Quay

Plage des Godelins

Pointe du
Sémaphore

Plage de la
Comtesse

D786

St-Quay-
Portrieux

Portrieux

Port d'Armor

④

steps

Plage du Moulin

Pointe du Vau Burel

③

Plage des Godelins

Le Vau
Chaperon

Pointe de
Trouquetet

⑦

Pointe de
Rognouze

②

②

Binic

Map 18 N
└ 1km ┘ ↑

Plage de
la Banche

Pointe de
Bréhin

Le Petit
Havre

Pointe
de
Pordic

①

※

⑥

Pordic

18/1 **CA** along
cliffs to Pointe
de Bréhin • Here
descend abruptly
to cross stream
• **CA** climbing to cliffs again
• Keep **R** at each junction till
first houses of Binic • At
abrupt end of path, take road
on **L** • Follow down to main road
(D786) and turn **R** • Shortly, turn **R**
down to P above Plage de la Banche
at Binic • Turn **L** along promenade,
then up the jetty on **R** • Cross over
little bridge at lock • Bear **R** and
CA along promenade to end of P
(before access to beach)

18/2 Turn **L** up zig-zag ramp
climbing cliff • **CA** 1km to skirt
Pointe de Rognouze • **CA** 500m to
Pointe de Trouquetet (with its
Corps de Garde) • Here turn
back **L** and descend to signpost
deep in valley • Turn **L** and **CA** up
path to hamlet of le Val Chaperon
• Turn **R** on Rue des Roches-Brunes
• Follow round bends to end • Here
follow footpath to steps down to
Plage des Godelins (bar/restaurant)
**the first of two beaches belonging
to the town of Étables-sur-Mer,
1km inland**

18/3 From Plage des Godelins, climb
access road to bend and take signed
path on **R** • Follow round Pointe du
Vau Burel to emerge at Étables'
second beach, the Plage du Moulin
(bar/restaurant) • **CA (keeping the**

Plage de la Comtesse

glorious white sandy beach on your R) to take road opposite • Follow this corniche road around headland • At sharp **L** bend, **CA** down steps on **R** to harbour at Portrieux

18/4 Bear **L** to walk along past harbour beach • Where road veers sharply **L** at deep water port, go up steps on **L** to white-fenced balcony path • Follow behind Plage de la Comtesse to Pointe du Semaphore

---

ST QUAY-PORTRIEUX

The founding father here was the 5th century Welsh monk St-Ké (sometimes thought to be the Sir Kay of the Arthurian legends) who arrived in a stone boat and was set upon by the local women. He owed his survival to the Virgin Mary, who created a spring to heal his wounds. Much revered, it is still in evidence today and can be seen near the Grève d'Isnain.

St Quay-Portrieux is really two towns joined together. St-Quay is a resort, gaining in popularity since the 1840s, when the local convent took pity on well-connected ladies whose health required sea-bathing therapy. Portrieux was a fishing port, whose men like so many others on this coast made frequent trips to the distant cod fields. Over the years the catch has been converted to mackerel and plaice – and scallops. Portrieux now claims itself to be the 'scallop capital' of France and on a winter's afternoon you can watch the shells being unloaded on the quayside. But times are still changing and the new deep water harbour here (Port d'Armor) is also home to around 1,000 pleasure craft.

SCALLOPS

A symbol of fertility to the Greeks, scallops took on another role in the Middle Ages when they became the emblem of St-James, and of the popular pilgrimage to his shrine at Santiago de Compostela. Every pilgrim carried one, and from this is derived the French name Coquilles St-Jacques. Scallop-eating is a relatively modern notion in that before the 19th century, they were regarded as no more than a last resort in time of famine. In recent years they have attained the status of a delicacy, and the restaurants of St-Quay-Portrieux can offer them baked, fried, steamed, poached, marinated, in sauces, in fricassées and a dozen other ways.

This new-found passion for scallops led in the 70s to a dramatic reduction in numbers, and a consequent need for regulations. Today, scallop fishing is confined to the winter months; it may take place on two days a week only, for no more than 45 minutes at a time, and with a dragnet of a certain mesh. All this ensures that scallops attain at least their reproductive age of 2 years before they are eaten, and that they are left in peace in the summer, at which time each hermaphrodite bivalve releases tens of millions of larvae into the sea. Hopefully scallops will never again be absent from the Bay of St-Brieuc, and visitors to St-Quay-Portrieux will be able to find them on the menu!

The **SEMAPHORE** is a coastguard lookout - this particular building was inaugurated in 1986. At the Point itself, a toposcope points out the St-Quay offshore archipelago, as well as more distant features of the horizon. Nearby is a monument to the crew of the 'Viking', nineteen young men who in the last World War attempted to cross the Channel to join the Free French Forces. They were caught off Nazi-occupied Jersey and most ended their lives in concentration camps.

• Beyond semaphore, **CA** to join main road in front of Casino, bearing **R** • Turn **R** in front of Bureau du Congrès • **CA** following balcony path around headland to little beach at Fonteny • **This is the beach at which St-Ké was said to have landed. His spring can be found by turning up the Rue de la Source**

Chapelle St-Marc

18/5 Climb to ⓟ and turn **R** to **CA** on coastal path • Pass campsites, and skirt sharp headland, **CA** to Plage St-Marc • **Just up the road here is the 15th century Chapelle** St-Marc • Cross ⓟ and **CA** on coastal path, climbing to splendid heights of Pointe du Bec de Vir with its table d'orientation • **CA** and down to restaurant and ⓟ at Port Goret • From ⓟ, ignore steps to beach, take path across field by benches with sea view • 500m descend to broad track (down to old harbour)

Pointe du Bec de Vir

• Follow **R** 20m, then turn **L** onto coastal path • **CA** along the cliff-top • **CA** through woodland and down log steps to wide track beside stone wall

19/1 Turn **R** here, descend to beach and turn **L** skirting pebbles to Le Palus (2 restaurants/crêperies, summertime buvette)

Le Pallus

• Cross ⓟ behind beach to steps just to **R** of restaurants • Climb through gorse and pine • At path junction, double back sharp **R** • **Happily the path assumes a more horizontal aspect as it rounds the cliff, and**

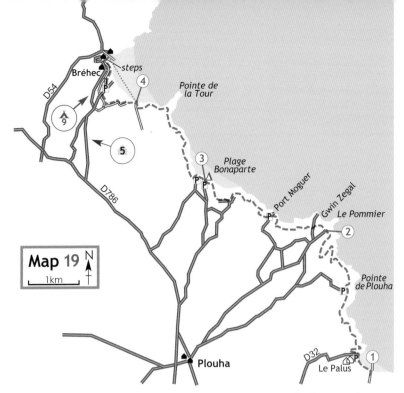

Map 19

ahead the Pointe de Plouha is in view, but the path dives and soars
more than once before reaching it. At a height of 104m, the
Pointe de Plouha is said to have the highest cliffs in Brittany • **CA**
on coastal path • Follow around broad sweeps inland up valleys, to
promontory of Le Pommier

19/2 **CA** here • 250m at road (leading down to harbour of Gwin Zegal)
turn **L** and almost immediately **R**

The harbour of Gwin Zegal is an example of one of the oldest types of
anchorage. Trees were once planted in the sand here, their roots secured
with heavy stones. Cut off at a height of around 10 metres, they now
provide secure mooring for boats. Look backwards from the path for a
good view of the picturesque scene.

Le Pommier

• **CA** on coastal path along cliff-top 750m • Follow **R** and descend to road at the creek of Port Moguer • Bear **R** aross road/ⓅP, then **L** on coast path • **CA** almost 1km, follow inland on hard-surfaced road • At **TJ** turn **R** • At end beside house, **CA** on track • Follow to memorial in large Ⓟ above Plage Bonaparte

OPERATION BONAPARTE

In 1944 this beach (then called the Anse de Cochat) was the theatre for Operation Bonaparte, the most successful evacuation of allied airmen stranded in France. Under the direction of the organisation known as Reseau Shelburne, such airmen were taken to secret houses in the vicinity of Plouha to wait. On hearing the coded radio message 'Bonjour tout le monde à la maison d'Alphonse', they were then smuggled to the home of Jean Gicquel, a member of the Plouha Resistance group, who lived a short distance from the beach. Later that night the men were led under cover of darkness down the steep cliff to the shore from where they were ferried to a waiting gun boat. Over several months, 135 men were returned in this way and no life was lost. The only casualty of the operation was the collecting house, the Maison d'Alphonse, eventually burned down by suspecting Nazis. Fortunately Jean Gicquel himself escaped the blaze and his wife and child had already long gone into hiding.

A simple plaque now marks the site of the Maison d'Alphonse. If you want to see it, walk up the road from the beach and take the first turning right – a total distance of about a kilometre. Just a little farther along the same road, the 15th century Chapelle St-Samson is also worthy of a visit.

Bréhec

19/3 From memorial, cross ⓟ and **CA** down to beach • Cross access road to path alongside stream, soon turning and climbing gently • At path junction, veer sharp **R** and **CA** up to cliff-top • **CA** to base of long rocky Pointe de la Tour • Bear **L** away from Point and **CA** until the path descends to a wider track • Turn **R** to back of beach

19/4 ALTERNATIVE: If the tide is out, you can now quickly walk around the shore to Bréhec, saving several circuitous kilometres • **MAIN ROUTE:** **CA** over hill, follow track inland • Before first house, turn sharp **R** onto wide track (former railway line) • At road turn **R** 100m to ⓟ on left • Cross ⓟ to lane leaving on far side • **CA** on grassy track (former railway again) and follow along cliff above town • At end by road, take flights of steps down to back of beach at Bréhec (restaurants)

Bréhec beach and harbour

6. PRACTICAL INFORMATION

SHOPS & SERVICES

- **St-Brieuc** TO 0825 00 22 22 www.baiedesaintbrieuc.com
- **Binic** TO 02 96 73 60 12 www.ville-binic.fr
- St-Quay-Portrieux TO 02 96 70 40 64 www.saintquayportrieux.com
- Plouha TO 02 96 20 24 73 www.plouha.com
- Les Rosaires

ACCOMMODATION

Chambres d'hôte

1. Mme Trehen (2km) Saint-Halory, 22590 Pordic 02 96 79 41 11 Open all year
2. Mme Lalot (100m) 13 Quai Jean Bart, 22520 Binic 02 96 73 69 00 Open all year
3. M Godme (100m) 3 rue Gen Leclerc, 22410 St-Quay-Portrieux 02 96 70 47 41
4. M. Jouany (400m) 3 rue Perhemeno, 22410 Treveneuc 02 96 70 59 08 jouany.andre@wanadoo.fr
5. Raymond Le Bars (1km) Kerdreux, 22580 Plouha 02 96 22 33 96

Camping

6. Camping le Roc de l'Hervieu (250m) 19, Rue d'Estienne d'Orves, 22590 Pordic 02 96 79 30 12 www.campinglerocdelhervieu.fr Open mid-May to September
7. Camping Les Fauvettes (on route) 13, Rue des Fauvettes, 22520 Binic 02 96 73 60 83 www.ville-binic.fr Open April to September
8. Camping Bellevue (on route) 22410 St-Quay-Portrieux 02 96 70 41 84 www.campingbellevue.net Open end April - mid-September
9. Camping le Varquez-sur-Mer (300m) 5 route de la Corniche Bréhec, 22580 Plouha 02 96 22 34 43 www.camping-le-varquez.com Open all year

TRANSPORT

Buses: Tibus no.9 St-Brieuc to Pointe de l'Arcouest - several buses a day stopping at Pordic, Binic, Étables, St-Quay-Portrieux and Bréhec. www.tibus.fr

TUB no.6 St-Brieuc to St-Laurent-Sur-Mer; TUB no.16 St-Brieuc to Les Rosaires. www.tubinfo.fr

Taxi: ´Allo Taxis 02 96 01 95 47 St-Brieuc

M. Batard 02 96 70 59 46 / 02 96 70 46 35 St-Quay-Portrieux

OTHER WALKS

A 6km circular walk named the Sentier des Falaises takes in the dramatic cliffs to the north of the Pointe de Plouha (details TO Plouha)

For a 8.5km circuit from Palus Plage walk up the coast to Le Pommier and return inland via Kerjean, Kerouziel and Kerraoult – yellow balisage, or for an 18km circuit go on to Plage Bonaparte, again returning by the inland route.

7. Bréhec - Lézardrieux

Trégor-Goëlo

47 kms

This section moves from the impressive high cliffs south of Paimpol to the gentle slopes of the estuary of the Trieux. In between are the villages of Arcouest, embarkation point for the popular île de Bréhat, and Loguivy, a time-warped little fishing port. The industry in both the Bay of Paimpol and the estuary is oyster-culture, and at low tide you can see tractor-loads of workers going out to tend the beds and the flat-bottomed boats racing home laden with sacks of oysters. On the north coast low tide is similarly revealing – a thousand tiny red-rock islands break through the turquoise waters. Largest of all is Bréhat, and it is well worth a diversion, although it is crowded in summertime. At the end of the section, Lézardrieux is an unremarkable town in a remarkable position. With a deep water harbour that has all-tide access, it hosts craft that would scarcely be out of place in St-Tropez!

Pointe de Minard

DIRECTIONS

20/1 At Bréhec, cross behind sandy beach to signed path up steps between houses on far side • Follow **R** up cliff • At path junction just before summit, bear **L** to road • Turn **R** and follow clifftop road 1.5kms • At sharp **L** bend take path on **R** • Follow down steeply to cove of Porz Pin, **renowned for its 'blue pebbles'** • At road turn **R**, then **L** to regain coastal path • Climb steeply to road and turn **R**

> **A ruined mill** stands starkly on the horizon here, one of 12 that once functioned in the vicinity. Of these, the Moulin de Craca (overlooking the bay, midway between Pointe de Bilfot and Pointe de Kerarzic) has been restored to grind corn once more and is open to visitors.

• Follow 1.2km to **TJ** and turn **R** • **CA** 500m to Pointe de Minard • Before P take grassy track on **L** • Descending to broader track, turn **L** and **CA** to **TJ** of tracks

20/2 100m turn **R** • At long flight of worn steps descend to creek of Porz Donan • At bottom bear **L** to cross plank bridge over stream • **CA** up to clifftop • At track junction bear **R** • **CA** 1km to road leading to Pointe de Plouézec (**now more often called the Pointe de Bilfot**) • **DIVERSION** (1.4kms): Turn **R**, follow road to point and return

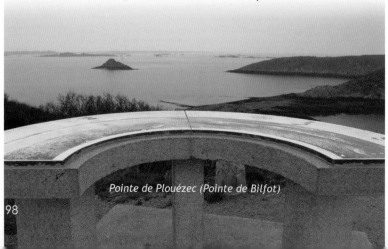

Pointe de Plouézec (Pointe de Bilfot)

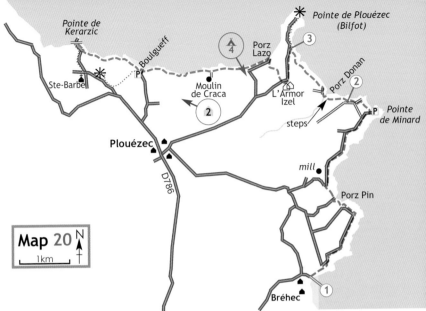

Map 20

POINTE DE BILFOT

Here there is a splendid ceramic orientation table identifying all the features of a fascinating stretch of coastline. A Resistance memorial stands nearby. The Point itself was apparently once an active volcano, the islands off its tip (Grand Mez de Goëlo, Petit Mez de Goëlo) mere outpourings of its lava.

On the way to the point, a sign on the left indicates the 'Panorama'. A path through the bushes leads to a possibly even better viewpoint overlooking the Bay of Paimpol. The modern statue here has no title, but the stricken face looking out to sea needs no interpretation.

20/3 At junction with road turn **L** • Follow 600m to hamlet of l'Armor Izel • After **R** bend, take track between houses on **R** • Follow down to Port Lazo at the foot of the cliff • Turn **L** on road beside bay • 250m find steps down on **R** • **CA** on coastal path 2.4kms (at 700m, diversion **L** via track to Moulin de Craca) • Cross P above beach of Boulgueff

PORZ LAZO

Porz Lazo, once a fishing port, now concerns itself only with the vast acres of oyster beds offshore. Its name is a corruption of the Breton Porz Lac'ho – Port of the Killing. In the 9th century, the local women apparently set fire to the English fleet here, killing all the crew.

Ste-Barbe orientation table

20/4 ALTERNATIVE (viewpoint and chapel at Ste-Barbe**):** Take grassy track along field edge behind Ⓟ • At road, turn **R** • 250m signed track on **R** leads to orientation table **with its tranquil view across the islands in the bay to Porz Even on the distant peninsula** • **CA** along road to 17th century Chapelle Ste Barbe on **L** • Follow lane opposite chapel down to Pointe de Kerarzic to rejoin main route

MAIN ROUTE: From Ⓟ above beach of Boulgueff **CA** on coastal path 1.25kms to road • Follow **R** down to Pointe de Kerarzic, **where there are oyster-culture premises**

21/1 Just above entrance to these, rejoin coastal path and **CA** into woodland • 700m descend to broad track • Turn **R** then **L** to cross stream (**Abbaye de Beauport ahead**)

ABBAYE DE BEAUPORT

The abbey was built in the 13th century by Count Alain de Penthièvre, and was given to a group of Premonstratensians from Normandy. Only the refectory was built later (14th century) and so it remains a pure classic example of the architecture of its time. It became an important halt on one of the pilgrim routes to Santiago de Compostela, and a stone bearing a coquille emblem stands outside. Monks were in residence at Beauport until the time of the Revolution, after which it was sold off. The abbey is open to the public daily and visits include the Gothic vaulted chapterhouse, the cloisters, the refectory and the visitors' accommodation. It can be accessed from the coastal path.

Tide mill at Kerity

• Follow track in front of abbey and along raised sea wall above marsh
• At road at Kerity **CA**, bearing **R** of lake • Follow **L** along dyke passing
restored tide mill • Beyond this, turn **R** past **P** and **R** again along path
above shore • At end, turn **L** between houses, then **R** to regain coastal
path • **CA** to Pointe de Guilben • **At the isthmus before the Point,
you can choose whether or not to circumnavigate the pine-clad
hillock at its tip** • From isthmus follow track on north side of
peninsula, bearing **R** at path junctions • **CA** along lowest part of cliff
to reach wide grassy track running above beach • At open grassy area
beside house, bear **R** under pines and descend steps • **CA** along wall
behind beach to port buildings at Paimpol

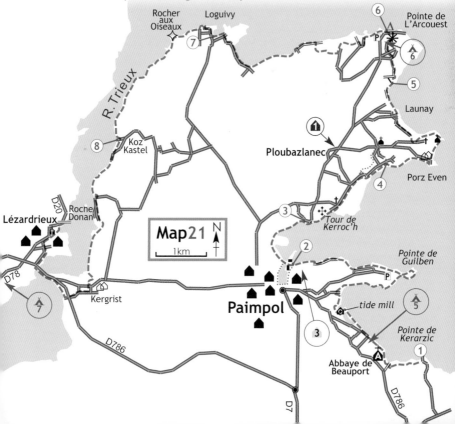

PAIMPOL

Paimpol is a town that once thrived on cod fishing, and from the 17th century onwards its menfolk would spend the summer months of every year off the coasts of Newfoundland or Iceland. That this was a dangerous occupation is reflected in the many local memorials, and in particular, in the cemetery wall at Ploubazlanec, where the names of those who did not return are recorded on plaques. The 1930s saw an end to it all, and today Paimpol's harbour boasts only a few inshore fishing boats, and many more pleasure craft.

Paimpol's piscatorial past is the focus of French writer Pierre Loti's book Pêcheur d'Islande (An Iceland Fisherman - available in translation). The town's other remembered son is Théodore Botrel, singer and poet of a century ago, whose statue stands in the Place de l'Église. He too gave the town a place in his repertoire (la Paimpolaise).

21/2 **ALTERNATIVES: EITHER**, if lock gates are closed, bear **R** here, cross lock gates, then footbridge · **OR**, if lock gates are open, or if desired, detour **L** around end of harbour (access to shops and restaurants) • **At the farthest corner of the port stands a granite monument on which the words of Charles de Gaulle honour the efforts of the merchant navy in the last World War** • From memorial **CA** behind wall, bearing **R** at its end to join rough road • Bear **L** then **R** around boat builders' premises, cross road directly and go through ℙ of Maison de la Mer to rejoin coastal path • **CA** on dyke across marsh, then alongside wall to meet road

21/3 **CA** in same direction, and at **L** bend **CA** on path passing below Tour de Kerroc'h, **a 19th century edifice peeping above the trees (and best seen from across the bay)** • Join road, **CA** to junction with curious calvary

THE CALVARY OF PLOUBAZLANEC (CALVAIRE CORNIC)

This unusual triangular calvary was erected at the beginning of the 18th century by Father Yves Cornic, and was intended to be the first Station of the Cross on the climb to a proposed chapel on the high promontory above Porz Even. The chapel was never finished, but its cross became the Croix des Veuves (widows' cross), still standing there today.

• From calvary, go ahead on Rue de Kerroc'h and **CA** 700m to fork

DIVERSION: fork **L** and **CA** on track (Chemin de Kergaud) climbing to village of Perros Hamon, **where there is an 18th century chapel with wide views across the bay. Inside are memorial plaques of men lost at sea.** At chapel take first **R**, 200m bear **L** and **CA** on track between houses to return to road at 21/4

MAIN ROUTE: fork **R**, follow **R** then **L** and **CA** on road 450m to 21/4

21/4 Take path on **R** (opposite, from diversion) dipping between houses

• Follow to fishing village of Porz Even • **CA** on road down to harbour

PORZ EVEN

A single street of 19th century fishermen's cottages leads down to the two harbours of Pors Even. On one side a jetty shelters the boats of the inshore fishers, while on the other, the road leads directly to the premises of the shellfish merchants. On the shore here you can see the claires (basins) where oysters spend their last days before reaching the table. Other granite-lined pits hold lobsters, crawfish and crabs waiting for collection. At low tide tractors come and go, and the flat-bottomed boats bring home the sacks of oysters.

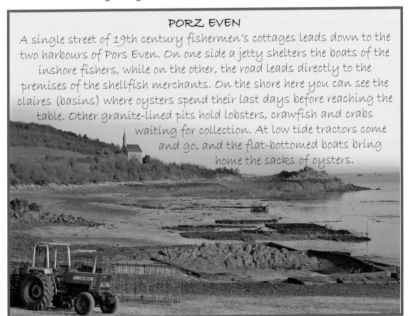

Île de Bréhat

• Returning from harbour, turn **R** (signed Chapelle de la Trinité) and **CA** on path • At chapel, **CA** following coast • Climb to road and turn **R** • **400m to the left at this point is the Croix des Veuves (Widows' Cross - see previous page), at a viewpoint where once anxious wives scanned the horizon for distant returning sails** • 20m take path downhill on **R** • At bottom **CA** on road 500m to take first road on **R (a well stands on the corner)** • Follow to back of beach at Launay • Turn **L** and **CA** along pebble bank to **CA** on clear track climbing at end

21/5 After skirting field, fork **R**, then turn **R** and immediately **L** (in front of property entrance) • **CA** on track becoming a tarmac road running between houses • At **TJ** turn **R** and immediately bear **L** on narrow Gardenn ar Spern Du • At junction, cross straight ahead onto Chemin du Rohou • Follow round to **R**, finally following signs **L** to Panorama • **At viewpoint the Île de Bréhat and all its archipelago**

ÎLE DE BRÉHAT

The pink-red outcrop of the île de Bréhat is actually two islands joined by a bridge, the whole being no more than 3 km from north to south. The islands are very different - the south boasts a rich vegetation of palms, fig trees and mimosa, while the north is more barren and wild.

A mere 300 people live on Bréhat all year round, but the wealth of hotels, holiday accommodation and second homes on the south island means that this number is increased ten times in the summer months. Also popular as a day-trip venue, the island can be almost 'standing room only' on a fine summer weekend. For those who decide to make the visit (15 minutes from l'Arcouest), there is no designated round-island walk, but the north island does have some fine sections of coastal path. Other attractions are a tide mill, 2 lighthouses, and some superb sea views - the very best from the top of a Buchanesque 39 steps leading to the Chapelle St-Michel.

are spread before you • Bear round to **L** on track descending under pines to road leading to embarcadère • Turn **L** on road, passing an interesting memorial

THE JOLIOT-CURIE MEMORIAL

Irène Curie, daughter of Marie and Pierre, was working at her mother's Radium Institute in Paris when she met fellow-worker Frédéric Joliot.

They married in 1926 and changed their names to Joliot-Curie. Continuing to work together in the fields of radioactivity and nuclear physics, in 1935 they were jointly awarded the Nobel Prize for Chemistry. The Joliot-Curies along with other Parisian intellectuals of the time frequently holidayed at Arcouest – which acquired the nickname 'Sorbonne Plage'.

21/6 **CA** on road and drop down to the car park on the **R** • At its far corner, find path along back of beach • 200m at road, turn **L** • Immediately past first house, take track on **R** • 100m turn **L** onto path along edge of wood • **CA** on track becoming road turning inland and climbing • In sight of houses at top, turn **R** on path between fields • In front of house gate, bear **R** to descend over steps and rocks to field below • Skirt field edge to reach track along back of beach • Turn **L** and follow track, becoming road, to **L** bend inland • Here **CA** 800m on path skirting coast to meet road by campsite • Following this road around the bay, you arrive at Loguivy • **CA** to end and descend steps on **R** to harbour

LOGUIVY

In the harbour of Loguivy the old fishing boats are now outnumbered by pleasure craft. Traditional fishing has largely been replaced by ostréiculture and the pursuit of crustaceans and molluscs such as crabs, crawfish and even Coquilles St-Jacques. A particular lobster known as the 'Bleu de Loguivy' is the pride of the catch.

Loguivy, with no beaches, remains relatively untouched by tourism – although it boasts that Lenin, worn out by 3 years hard work, recuperated here for a whole month in the summer of 1902.

105

Rocher aux oiseaux

21/7 Continue **R** around harbour then ahead on narrow road • Follow **L**, then sharp **R** between hedge and wall to back of beach • Turn **L** and cross access road to **CA** on coastal path • Down steps, turn sharp **L** along back of sailing school, then **L** again up steps • Follow path inland and up long flight of log steps to Rocher aux Oiseaux

ROCHER AUX OISEAUX This outcrop of rock commanding the entrance to the Trieux estuary is known to have been favoured by prehistoric man. Primitive tools cut from the rock itself date back some 5000 years. There is a fine view of the estuary, its oyster beds visible at low tide.

• Follow log steps down and **CA** • **Another two serious climbs follow then suddenly tranquillity returns and the path meekly runs through woodland above the river, passing an old lime kiln that was once fuelled by oyster shells** • Descend to beach at Koz Kastel

21/8 CA along dyke of former tide mill and up access road • Behind stone house, **CA** on coastal path on **R** • 800m, at slipway at Roche Donan, turn **R** on road • Pass ℗ to **CA** on upper road above seafaring school • **Good views of Roche Donan itself – a long raised bar of rock that almost closes the estuary** • Turn **L** up steps and **CA** on coastal path through woods above R.Trieux • Drop down to beach, then return to woods and follow inland to clearing beside lavoir • Bear **R** and climb to main road in Kergrist • Cross over and **CA** 100m to **TJ**, turn **R**

Trieux estuary

Roche Donan

In Kergrist lived Yves le Cor, principle character in Pierre Loti's novel *Mon Frère Yves*. Pierre Loti (alias Louis Marie Julie Viaud), naval captain turned author, was considered France's best descriptive writer of the late 19th century. Born in Rochefort, his novels have a maritime flavour and many have been translated into English.

• Bear **L** beside houses to pass under D786 • Just before beach, take path on **R** along edge of fields to main road near river bridge • Cross this and take first **R** into Lézardrieux • Go straight over at the cross-roads and turn **R** in the centre of town in front of the Post Office •
• In front of church, fork **R** • Cross **P** to path descending through conifers to back of harbour • Walk **L** around harbour and **CA** on D20 leaving Lézardrieux

---

LÉZARDRIEUX

The name Lézardrieux comes from the Breton Léh ar Tréon, meaning Place of the Trieux, and in crossing the bridge into town you are entering the territory known as Trégor. The bridge itself, built in 1924, is the earliest example of a cable-stayed bridge in France. The most noteworthy building in Lézardrieux is its church with a gabled belfry. It is on the marked route of the coastal path, so can be easily admired – but there are others similar in the vicinity.

Bridge into Lézardrieux

7. PRACTICAL INFORMATION

SHOPS & SERVICES

- Plouézec (2km) TO 02 96 22 72 92 (summer only) www.plouezec.fr Mkt Sat
- Paimpol TO 02 96 20 83 16 www.paimpol-goelo.com Mkt Tues am
- Ploubazlanec (1.5km) Mkt Sun am
- Loguivy
- Lézardrieux TO (out of town on D786 west) 02 96 22 16 45 www.lezardrieux.com Mkt Fri

ACCOMMODATION

Rand' Hôtel (particularly geared to the needs of walkers)

1. Rand' Hôtel Les Agapanthas (800m) 1, Rue Adrien Rebous, 22620 Ploubazlanec 02 96 55 89 06 www.hotel-les-agapanthas.com

Chambres d'Hôte

2. Mme Le Hoguillard (500m) 3 Hent Prat Coutel, 22470 Plouézec 02 96 22 70 50 http://pagesperso-orange.fr/3prat-coutel
3. Mme Melo (100m) 'La boite à sardines ruz', 15 rue de la Tossen, 22500 Paimpol 02 96 20 48 36 http://monsite.wanadoo.fr/dormirapaimpol

Camping

4. Camping Le Cap Horn (200m) Port Lazo, 22470 Plouézec 02 96 20 64 28 www.lecaphorn.com Open late March - late October
5. Camping Municipal de Cruckin (on route) rue de Cruckin, 22500 Paimpol 02 96 20 78 47 www.camping-paimpol.fr Open April - Oct
6. Camping Panorama du Rohou (100m) Pointe de l'Arcouest, 22620 Ploubazlanec 02 96 55 87 22 www.campingpanorama.com Open all year
7. Camping Municipal de Kermarquer (300m) 23 rue de Kermarquer, 22740 Lézardrieux 02 96 20 17 22 Open mid-June to mid-September

TRANSPORT

Bus services: no.9 Bréhec - Paimpol; also Paimpol to Arcouest (Bréhec to Arcouest entails a change in Paimpol). No. 7 Paimpol - Lézardrieux (10 minutes on the bus and a 25km walk) on www.tibus.fr

Taxi: Taxi Omnès 02 96 20 58 02 / 06 07 48 37 09 Ploubazlanec Taxi Lézardrieux 02 96 20 58 02 / 02 96 20 15 00 Lézardrieux

Ferry to Bréhat: Les vedettes de Bréhat, 6 route embarcadère, 22620 Ploubazlanec 02 96 55 79 50 www.vedettesdebrehat.com

OTHER WALKS

With the aid of buses, day walks are possible between Bréhec and Paimpol and between Paimpol and Arcouest.

8. Lézardrieux-Tréguier
Presqu'île Sauvage
39 kms

The peaceful river estuaries at the beginning and end of this section contrast sharply with the wild north coast in between. As the tide falls, emerging stones, rocks, reefs and craggy islands make it difficult to tell where the land ends and the sea begins. Most impressive of all is the Sillon de Talbert, a 3km long pebble bank projecting from the north-east corner. Its tip is technically the most northerly point in Brittany.

The Sillon de Talbert has a certain tourist appeal, and the village of le Québo at its foot is the only village of any note on the whole coast. The banks of the Trieux at the beginning and the Jaudy at the end can boast little more, making this a very rural walk. Even so, it is a popular one, as evinced by the many car parks and children's play areas along the coast. You are most unlikely to have the path to yourself on a fine weekend at any time in the year!

At the end of the section, Tréguier, on the Jaudy estuary, is a most characterful town. Elegantly-spired cathedral, colourful half-timbered buildings and a vibrant port make it worthy of at least a short pause in anyone's journey.

View down the Trieux

DIRECTIONS

22/1 From D20, take signed flight of steps descending **R** to beach (this energetic diversion is to take you off the main road) • **CA** up beach access road • **This is named Rue Georges Brassens – the celebrated French singer owned No.4 from 1971 to 1980** • At main road, take road immediately on **R** • **CA** on broad track through woodland above estuary • Follow zig-zag down to river • At last bend, take track **L** into valley (information boards describe the birds and wildlife here) • **CA** on track out of valley • At road turn **L** • Pass lighthouse of Coat Mer Amont (**one of many defining the channel of the Trieux**) • Take broad track on **R** before farm • **CA** skirting field and descend through woodland • At road in valley turn **L**, then **R** to ruined tide mill • Pass tide mill and **CA** ahead on shore 100m (**This may not be possible at very high tide, in which case go back up road to main road, turn R - crêperie on corner - and take first R to rejoin main route at Kerhamon**)

22/2 Turn **L** alongside stream and climb up lush green valley • At hamlet of Coalan, turn **R** and **CA** on road • At **TJ** turn **R** • In hamlet of Kerhamon bear **R** then **L** to rough track opposite between two farms • At tarmac road in hamlet of Prat turn **R** and follow 400m (to start of descent) and take track on **L** • Follow **L** and at fork go **R** • At road turn **R** and follow 1km to village of Kermouster

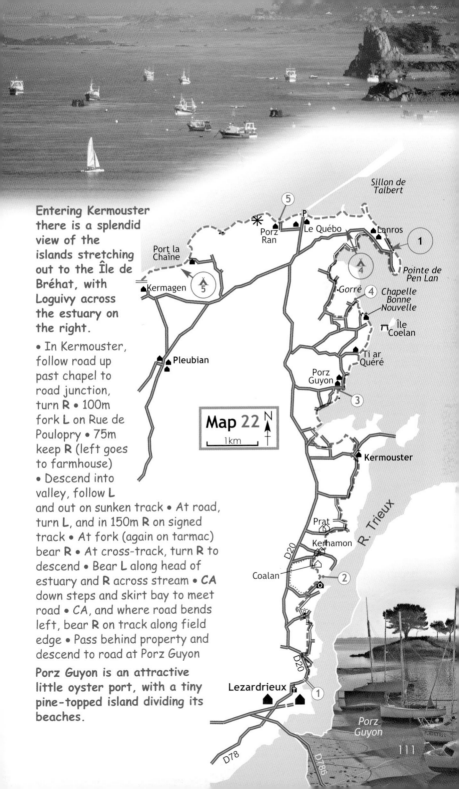

Entering Kermouster there is a splendid view of the islands stretching out to the Île de Bréhat, with Loguivy across the estuary on the right.

• In Kermouster, follow road up past chapel to road junction, turn **R** • 100m fork **L** on Rue de Poulopry • 75m keep **R** (left goes to farmhouse)
• Descend into valley, follow **L** and out on sunken track • At road, turn **L**, and in 150m **R** on signed track • At fork (again on tarmac) bear **R** • At cross-track, turn **R** to descend • Bear **L** along head of estuary and **R** across stream • **CA** down steps and skirt bay to meet road • **CA**, and where road bends left, bear **R** on track along field edge • Pass behind property and descend to road at Porz Guyon

Porz Guyon is an attractive little oyster port, with a tiny pine-topped island dividing its beaches.

Sillon de Talbert

Porz Ran

Le Québo

Lanros

Pointe de Pen Lan

Port la Chaîne

Kermagen

Gorré

Chapelle Bonne Nouvelle

Île Coelan

Pleubian

Ti ar Quéré

Porz Guyon

Map 22 N
1km

Kermouster

R. Trieux

Prat

Kerhamon

Coalan

Lezardrieux

Porz Guyon

D20

D78

D786

111

22/3 Turn **R** and follow road through Porz Guyon • At top of hill bear **R** on track alongside field • Bear **L** to skirt bay • At next oyster port, Ti ar Quéré, follow down to beach • Cross to end of access road, and **CA** along raised bank, **soon passing sandy bays with views to the Île Coalen and, farther away, the Point of Pen-Lan**

The Île Coalen is accessible at low tide. At its southern tip is a gallery grave (allée couverte) dating from the Neolithic period.

• **CA** on or near shore almost 1km to Chapelle Bonne Nouvelle

• Pass through chapel compound to sunken lane • Turn **L** and **CA** to

CHAPELLE BONNE NOUVELLE

The name means 'Chapel of Good News'. Built in the 16th century, it is still in use and is a place of pilgrimage for young women wishing to conceive.

road • Bear **R** and immediately past house on right, turn **R** beside bank along field edge • At far corner, bear **L** through gap to next field, then **R** through another gap • **CA** beside hedge, then bear **L** to reach broad track

22/4 Follow track to road junction and **CA** on road opposite • At top of hill, turn **R** on track (passing an obvious converted mill) • At road turn **R** • At TJ turn **R** • After farm of Gorré, fork **L** • Where road swings left, **CA** on wide track to marsh • Initially bear **L**, then **CA** bearing **R** to follow edge of marsh 1km • At road in Lanros bear **R** and follow to Pointe de Pen-Lan • **CA** right to end and bear **L** to continue on coastal path

Marais near Lanros

POINTE DE PEN LAN

The business premises at the point are largely concerned with the commercial uses of seaweed. Visible from the path, the Maison de l'Algue is a resource centre and exhibition area, open to visitors from mid-June to mid-September.

- Past ostreiculture premises, join Rue du Sillon Noir and **CA** to its end
- **CA** around headland, then around back of beach • Join track beside house and bear **R** to continue around bay • Finally climb steps to **P** at le Québo (restaurant) • From behind restaurant at start of Sillon **CA** on coast path to next beach, Porz Ran

THE SILLON DE TALBERT

This 3km long spit of sand and shingle is the result of meeting currents from the estuaries of the Trieux and the Jaudy. Known to have been 6km long and much higher in the 18th century, it seems that the Sillon is slowly disappearing. Don't miss this opportunity to take a walk out to its tip (although note that it is also a haven for seabirds, and may be closed off at nesting time).

Sillon de Talbert

Near Port La Chaîne

PORZ RAN AND THE VIEWPOINT OF CREAC'H MAOUT

On the hill above Porz Ran, the old semaphore turned blockhaus tells the terrible tale of the massacre of August 1944, when local residents defied a remaining outpost of Nazi soldiers. On a brighter note, a new toposcope has been erected on the site, its view comprising the Sillon de Talbert and a host of islands out to sea. Beyond the Sillon can be seen the Phare des Héaux. The site of Creac'h Maout can be reached in about 10 minutes from Porz Ran (see below).

22/5 **CA** from Porz Ran, pass playground and climb steps to **CA** round headland (access to Creac'h Maout on **L** after steps) • 800m path bears inland behind house, then turns **R** to descend between houses to beach • Cross head of beach to path up cliff • **CA** around headland to road at Port la Chaîne • Cross playground, and go **R** of house to **CA** on long pebble bank • Beyond this, follow briefly inland behind rock outcrop, then descend to seafront at Kermagen

KERMAGEN AND PLEUBIAN

Kermagen is an outpost of Pleubian, 1.5 kms on the road south. Its pride and joy is the 16th century chaire à prêcher or outdoor pulpit. The huge circular granite structure was moved from its original position in the old cemetery of Pleubian to stand beside the church. Its well preserved carvings depict the Passion of Christ, including the Last Supper and are considered an early role-model for the decorated calvaries of the region.

Port Béni

23/1 CA on road, passing playground and campsite • **CA** on broad track behind beach 1.5km to hamlet of St-Laurent, just before next visible headland • At road in St-Laurent, bear **R** on coastal path • **CA** round headland (**very popular with weekend strollers**) and descend to rock-strewn shores of Port Béni • Pass playground (**this area seems to be particularly well supplied**) and **CA** on road to jetty • After this go down onto beach and bear **L** behind hedge to **CA** on coastal path, now skirting fields above bay • At end go down steps and turn **L** on track to reach road

23/2 Turn **R** on road, **CA** 500m • At sharp left bend, **CA** on hedge-lined track to **TJ**

DIVERSION: to **R** here is the Allée Couverte de Men ar Rompet

MAIN ROUTE: at **TJ** turn **L**, then **R** on road to **P** behind beach • **CA** to beach, turn **L**, and (ignoring waymarks) **CA** on beach 800m

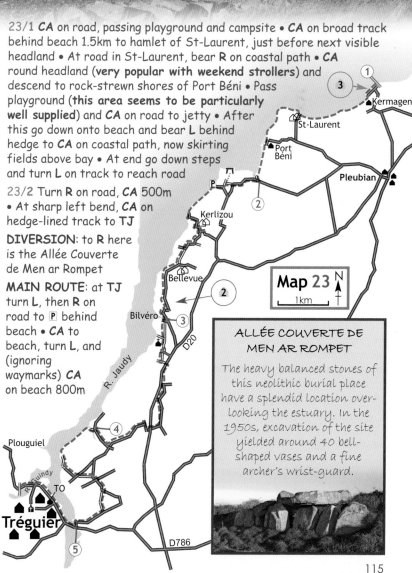

Map 23

1km   N

ALLÉE COUVERTE DE MEN AR ROMPET

The heavy balanced stones of this neolithic burial place have a splendid location overlooking the estuary. In the 1950s, excavation of the site yielded around 40 bell-shaped vases and a fine archer's wrist-guard.

Bilvéro harbour

• Just beyond pine plantation join road and follow inland to hamlet of Kerlizou • At next junction, keep **R**, and soon go **R** again (track on left) • At fork where tarmac road dips to right, **CA** on gravelled track to hamlet of Bellevue • Turn **R** on road and follow 1km, down to **TJ**

23/3 Turn **R** (harbour of Bilvéro ahead), and take track climbing behind stone house on **L** • **CA** as track becomes sunken lane and joins track from estuary • Follow past Chapelle St-Votrom

CHAPELLE ST-VOTROM

Votrom is said to have been a healer in the pre-Christian era, later venerated. This 16th century chapel dedicated to the saint has recently been restored.

• At road, turn **R** and immediately **L** beside house (ignore waymarks) • Turn **L** to reach main road (**The D20 can be busy, and the route avoids it as much as possible**) • Turn **R** and follow D20 300m • Turn **L** and immediately fork **R** (road parallel to D20, the old road) • Just before main road again, go **L** and follow to take first **R**. • Cross D20 to road directly opposite, immediately bear **R**, then follow **L** • At crossroads in 1km, turn **R**

23/4 At right bend and beginning of steep descent, take rough track **L**, down through woods • Turn **L** to cross stream, **CA** down to shore • **CA** over stones and seaweed 800m to track along back of beach • **CA** on access road leading past farm to **TJ** • Go **L**, then immediately bear **R** on track • At road, turn **R**, then at cross-roads **CA** • 250m later, at left bend, take track on **R** • At road, turn **R** and **CA** 500m to river bank **beside ruins of medieval bridge** • Turn **L** , then **R** across suspension bridge over R. Jaudy into Tréguier

23/5 Over bridge take first road **R** • **CA** past port **and TO housed in the handsome Tours d'Armateurs. The road uphill beside the Tourist Office - Rue Ernest Renan - leads to the central square and the cathedral** • From Tourist Office **CA** beside river • Bear **R** across bridge over R. Guindy, leaving Tréguier for Plouguiel

TRÉGUIER

Founded by St-Tugdual, a Welsh saint arriving here in the 6th century, Tréguier is one of the seven original bishoprics of Brittany. The town's physical and spiritual heart is its cathedral, whose pink granite spire, so pierced that it appears almost latticed, towers a dizzy 63 metres over the square below. The cathedral itself is a blend of many centuries of ecclesiastical architecture and boasts Renaissance choir stalls, some fine stained glass windows and elegant 15th century cloisters. Most importantly it contains the tomb of St-Yves, a great favourite with Bretons. Born locally, Yves Helori de Kermartin was a 13th century lawyer, judge and advocate for the poor, who ultimately abandoned his profession to enter the church. St-Yves is now considered the patron saint of lawyers, and from all over the world they descend on Tréguier for the day of his pardon, the 3rd Sunday in May. Law societies of France, Belgium and the United States have donated windows to his chapel.

Around the cathedral, the Place du Martray is flanked by cheerfully coloured half-timbered houses and there are many more in the narrow streets beyond. The statue of native philosopher Ernest Renan so close to the cathedral has in its time sparked much controversy – his books questioned the most fundamental tenets of Christianity. His birthplace and childhood home is now a museum.

Down on the quayside, the Tours d'Armateurs that house the Tourist Office were once grain stores on a busy commercial wharf. Today there is little trade left and pleasure craft dominate the deep water moorings.

8. PRACTICAL INFORMATION

SHOPS & SERVICES

- **Lézardrieux** TO 02 96 22 16 45 www.lezardrieux.com Mkt Fri
- **Pleubian** TO 02 96 22 17 36 Mkt Sat
- **Tréguier** TO 02 96 92 22 33 www.ot-cotedesajoncs.com Mkt Wed
- Le Québo (restaurant/tabac inland on main road, open all year)

ACCOMMODATION

Chambres d'hôte

1. M et Mme Bouchon (on route) 18, Rue des Goémonniers, Lanros
   02 96 22 87 30 Open all year
2. Roselyne MERCIER et Jean-Claude MIGNON (150m) 11 Crec'h Arhant,
   22610 Kerbors 02 96 55 54 60 rose.mercier@club-internet.fr
   http://rose.mercier.club.fr/chambre

Rando-Gîte

3. Rando Gîte de Kermagen (on route) 98 Kermagen, 22610 Pleubian
   02 96 22 92 02 / 06 82 17 88 88

Camping

4. Camping Municipal de Lanros (250m) Lanros, 22610 Pleubian
   02 96 22 99 11 Open July to early September
5. Camping Port la Chaîne (on route) 22610 Pleubian 02 96 22 92 38
   www.portlachaine.com Open April to mid-October
6. Camping Municipal Kermagen (on route) 22610 Pleubian
   02 96 22 99 45 Open July and August only

TRANSPORT

Buses: Several buses a day connect Lézardrieux and Tréguier directly,
but only the very occasional bus makes its way between Pleubian
(Lanros) and Lézardrieux. Check both times and days of the week
carefully before relying on it. www.tibus.fr (route no 7)

Taxi: Taxi Macé 02 96 92 93 95 Tréguier
Taxi Trégorroisr 02 96 92 31 78 Minihy-Tréguier
Taxi Briand 02 96 92 49 00 Minihy-Tréguier

OTHER WALKS

For linear day-walks on this peninsula
you will almost certainly need a taxi as
buses are infrequent. But the number
of car parks on the north coast makes
it very accessible, and if you are happy
to walk 'out and back' it is certainly an
interesting stretch to explore.

Local TOs can offer a selection of
waymarked walks in the area. See also
the TO websites above.

9. Tréguier - Perros-Guirec
La Côte des Ajoncs
50 kms

This section begins on the quiet unpopulated banks of the Jaudy estuary and ends on the busy modern seafront of Trestraou in Perros-Guirec. The transition is a gradual one. The lonely banks and little oyster ports of the early stages are succeeded by the relatively unsophisticated attractions of the Pointe du Château - a roaring chasm in the rocks, a house sandwiched between boulders and an information point in the Maison du Littoral. The coast beyond is wild and rocky, no place for sandcastles or sunbathing, but the sands of the Anse de Gouermel give the first hint of what is to come. Pretty Bugélès is followed by Port Blanc, where the holiday beaches and attendant campsites really begin. The splendid arc of sand at Trestel gives way to a particularly lovely wooded stretch that ends at the approach to Perros-Guirec. Even here you are introduced gently to the pace of a modern holiday resort - the first beach, Trestrignel, is ringed by extravagant villas of the 1890s. Around the headland, the family-friendly sands of Trestraou are backed by restaurants, bars and a casino, and the metamorphosis is complete!

DIRECTIONS

24/1 After crossing R. Guindy in Tréguier, follow main road **L** • Take first road **L** (no-through-road) • **CA** down to river, and turn **R** on **pleasant tree-shaded path** • Join road, **CA** to junction and turn **R** • Half way up steep hill, turn sharp **R** and follow, bearing **L**, to main road in Plouguiel

PLOUGUIEL *derives its name from the Breton saint Kiel, the 'Plou' that is so common in these parts simply meaning 'parish'. So close to Tréguier, Plouguiel too has its roots in Christianity, and there are more than 20 wayside calvaries in the area. At one time, 15 watermills turned on the Guindy, and Plouguiel had its own port to export the grain.*

• Turn **L**, follow 100m • At left bend, **CA** • Turn **R** at **TJ**, then **R** again at calvary (signed Beg Melen) • **CA** 1.5km to cross-roads, turn **R** down to hamlet of Crec'h Suillet • Follow to shore, then head north (**L**), **negotiating seaweed, rocks, entrant streams and mud** • 500m at inlet **CA** on path at back of beach • Follow to harbour at La Pointe Jaune

24/2 Go **R** on road, **CA** on beach • 50m beyond house take grassy track **L** • After zig-zagging uphill, bear **L** to road • Turn **R**, **CA** 200m then turn **R** • **CA** through le Golot • **CA** 500m and bear **L** (ignore waymarks) to **TJ** and turn **R** • **CA** on 'main' road through La Roche Jaune

Harbour at La Pointe Jaune

Islands at low tide, from Le Palud

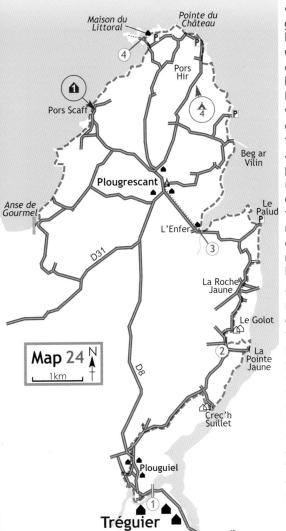

Maison du Littoral
Pointe du Château
④
Pors Hir
Pors Scaff
④
P
P
P
Beg ar Vilin
Plougrescant
Anse de Gourmel
Le Palud
P
L'Enfer
③
La Roche Jaune
D31
Le Golot
②
La Pointe Jaune
Map 24 N
1km
Crec'h Suillet
D8
Plouguiel
①
Tréguier

• The first turning **R** goes down to the harbour for those who want to explore - and a steep alleyway just before the harbour leads to the local viewpoint - a prospect of rocks and islands at the mouth of the Jaudy. This old fishing port now concerns itself more with the oyster industry, and the provision of moorings for pleasure craft. There is a restaurant on the harbourside

• 500m take track **R** returning to estuary and coastal path • Cross through oyster culture premises and **CA** on path to **P** of le Palud

• Go **L** up access road then **R** along coastal path • Follow round rock-strewn coast to point • **CA** to road again at l'Enfer (**Hell** - but there seems nothing devilish about this pretty spot)

Baie d'Enfer

DIVERSION: from bridge at l'Enfer, **CA** up road 1km to village of Plougrescant (shops and restaurants)

PLOUGRESCANT

Here is the Chapel of St-Gonéry, a curious Romanesque edifice that leans as if it had been pushed sideways. To add to its bizarre appearance, a leaded spire bristling with gargoyles was added to the tower in the 17th century. The weight of the lead has since caused the whole structure to buckle and bend in the middle, and the spire no longer points to heaven. Notwithstanding all this, the chapel has certain treasures (that can only be viewed on guided visits), most remarkable of which are the Old and New Testament scenes painted on the wooden ceiling. Naturally it contains the tomb of St-Gonéry, a 6th century Irish druid and healer who evangelised this area.

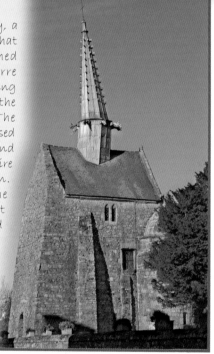

24/3 At l'Enfer, cross road bridge, walk uphill a few paces and take track behind barrier on **R** (**NOT the track along the shore**) • Follow through woodland beside estuary, emerging beside field and descending to beach • Bear **L** and **CA** on coast path to harbour of Beg ar Vilin

In the harbour of **BEG AR VILIN**, new boats are moored beside stark skeletons of the old. The long spit of land that provides shelter for them all is now given over to a municipal camp site.

- At road turn **L**, and very shortly go **R** on coastal path beside fence of oyster farming establishment • **CA** through next **P**, go **L** on access road, and take steps **R** up bank onto coastal path • **This particularly lovely stretch of path continues without interruption (other than a couple of access roads) almost all the way to Pointe du Château** • With houses of Pors Hir ahead, follow path left around field to meet road • Turn **R**, then bear **R** and **CA** to beach and jetty • **CA** past **P** and take track **R**, rounding headland and returning to road • Keep to **R** on narrow road (for *riverains* only - those who live here) • Pass to **L** of low stone cottages • **CA** between properties, then bear **R**, coming between rocks to open area in hollow behind beach • Bear **R** onto grassy track, passing beneath pine trees, then through old gate posts to conservation area of heathland

Near Pors Hir

Pointe du Château

Le Gouffre

CASTEL MEUR

The Maison du Littoral provides exhibitions and information about this wild coast and organises walks and other events exploring the natural environment. Just beyond the Maison is a classic scene that has appeared in innumerable tourist brochures and Brittany guides – across a lake, a pretty granite house is flanked by two huge rocks forming the side walls. The house was built almost a hundred and fifty years ago, when tourists with cameras were undreamt of. Today the owner has had to make a formal request for privacy.

• **From the summit of this there are impressive views of the barren rocky coast ahead.** • Descend to site known as Castel Meur, ignore P, and bear **R** to Maison du Littoral • **CA** past lake to road and turn **L**

24/4 **DIVERSION: A right turn here will take you out to the Gouffre, a huge chasm in the rock in the depths of which the sea thunders and roars on a stormy day**

• **CA** on road, bearing **R** at barrier onto path behind first house
• Follow along rocky coast 2km to road at Pors Scaff (**Huge rocks greet your entry to Pors Scaff. The three in a line have been named The Needles and beyond them is the Rocher de Napoléon, a reference to his bicorne hat**)

Near Bugélès

• **CA** on road to take first road **R** • Almost immediately bear **R** onto coastal path • **With views of innumerable rocky islets, and houses tucked between rocks** • **CA** to horseshoe bay of Anse de Gouermel (restaurant)

25/1 **CA** on road • Follow up from bay, then take track **R** • Follow down to beach • **CA** on beach into Bugélès (at high tide walk along field edge behind) • At beach access road **CA**, passing **R** of house on rocks and cutting across next headland by passing through two gaps in hedges • Cross last stretch of beach to reach road to harbour • Turn **L** on harbour road (leaving harbour on **R**) and **CA** through village as far as

BUGÉLÈS

The seascapes at Bugélès are amazing. The village is situated on a promontory ringed with islands, most of which are privately owned and therefore inaccessible. The largest island, St-Gilda's, has an 11th century chapel that welcomes visitors to its Pardon on just one day each year. The story behind it is that many, many years ago, a terrible illness wiped out all the horses in the area. The only ones to survive were those on St-Gilda's – and obviously this was due to the protection of the saint. Since that time, pilgrims have come to St-Gilda's to ask a blessing on their horses. The animals gallop through the waters at low tide, while visitors not on horseback come by tractor, boat or any other means they can find.

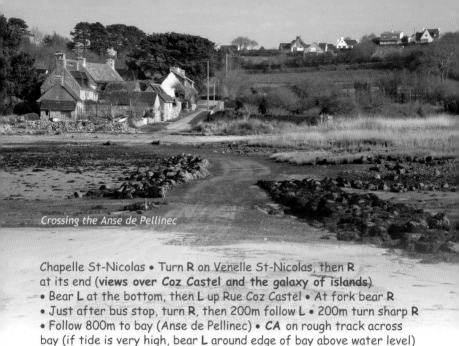

Crossing the Anse de Pellinec

Chapelle St-Nicolas • Turn **R** on Venelle St-Nicolas, then **R** at its end (**views over Coz Castel and the galaxy of islands**) • Bear **L** at the bottom, then **L** up Rue Coz Castel • At fork bear **R** • Just after bus stop, turn **R**, then 200m follow **L** • 200m turn sharp **R** • Follow 800m to bay (Anse de Pellinec) • **CA** on rough track across bay (if tide is very high, bear **L** around edge of bay above water level)

25/2 At road junction turn **R** • Almost at hilltop turn **R** • At left bend take green path on **R** (ignore waymarks) • Follow straight down to coast and turn **L** on coast path to port of Port Blanc • **CA** past port and, keeping **R**, **CA** along promenade

Chapelle St-Nicolas

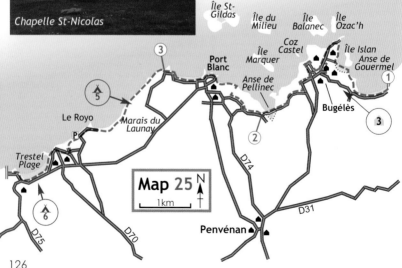

PORT BLANC

Named from the white pebbles of its beach, Port Blanc's most postcard-worthy feature is a huge rock stack topped by an oratory, the Rocher de la Sentinelle. With a commanding view of the sea and the islands, the building was originally designed as a watch tower – the statue of the Virgin was added at a much later date.

25/3 At far end of seafront road **CA** on coast path, passing campsite • **CA** on grassy bank above beach to le Royo • **To the left is the Marais du Launay, a low-lying area criss-crossed by drainage channels and now partly wooded** • **CA** on road, cross Ⓟ, then **CA** along fence beside property • Join end of road and **CA** to **TJ** • Turn **R** and **R** again at main road • Follow towards sea • At bottom **CA** between buildings and bear **L** down ramp to beach (Trestel Plage) • Cross beach to steps up to promenade • **CA** along behind beach and after road starts to climb, take first road **R** (signed Port le Goff)

TRESTEL PLAGE

The development of Trestel Plage began in 1929 when a sanatorium was built here to take advantage of the sea air in a bay sheltered from harsh breezes. After such a recommendation, private houses were soon built nearby and today holiday apartments, a camp site and a couple of restaurants have been added along the beach road.

26/1 At road end by little stony beach of Port le Goff, take broad track **L** between grassy banks, soon climbing into woodland • **Views of the long bare uninhabited rock of Île Tomé. Birds nest now where pirates and corsairs once had their hide-outs.**

Near Kerie

• At hamlet of Kerie, turn **L** on rough lane, then take second **R**, passing through 🅿 • *CA* on track to first houses of Port l'Épine • Leave pebble bank for tarmac road on **L** (camp site on right) • Follow road to 🅿 on seafront at Port l'Épine

PORT L'ÉPINE

Today the stony beach of Port l'Épine is sandwiched between two campsites, and only a handful of boats take advantage of the mooring behind its jetty. In the Anglo-French conflicts of the 18th century, the headland here was the site of an important battery guarding the bay of Perros-Guirec. Later used by customs officers, its remains can still be seen on the southern tip.

Île Tomé

Pointe du Sphinx
Port Le Goff
①
Palais des Congrès
Plage de Trestrignel
Pointe du Château
Kerie
⑥
Plage de Trestraou
④ 7
Port l'Epine
🅿
Palais des Congrès
🅿
②
⑤
Pointe du Château

Perros-Guirec
④ 9

Plage des Arcades

Map 26 N
1km

Nantouar
🅿

④
marina
③ 🅿
D75

Pont ar Sauz
② Truzugal ▲
④ 8 Louannec
D788
D6
D38

128

Lighthouse at Nantouar

26/2 From P bear **L** on road signed Pors Garo, Louannec • **CA** on grassy track • Just before beach, go up steps on **L** to **CA** around coast • At fork bear **R**, descending to P at Nantouar • **CA** on pebble bank • **CA** passing in front of lighthouse • Cross slipway and **CA** through woodland to meet road below P in Louannec

LOUANNEC The town itself is on the hill above, a walk of about 500m. St-Yves was once parish priest of Louannec – the church contains a 15th century wood carving depicting the saint.

26/3 30m up access road take path **R** climbing into wood • 1km follow inland across stream to road • Turn **R** and then **L** at the beach, alongside campsite • At end turn **L** to skirt harbour at Truzugal, **CA** to main road (D6) • Turn **R** beside road, and at roundabout at Pont ar Sauz (**the entry to Perros-Guirec**), bear **R** to **CA** across grassland behind beach • Rejoin road, bear **R** to go round marina • **This huge marina has moorings for more than 800 boats, a mere tenth of them for visitors**

Perros Guirec

129

PERROS-GUIREC

Perros Guirec has three main beaches, the Beach of the Arcades facing east and those of Trestrignel and Trestraou facing north. Each has its own character – Les Arcades is undeveloped, Trestrignel is surrounded by Belle Époque villas, while Trestraou has as its backdrop the Casino, Palais des Congrès and modern thalassotherapy centre. The centre of town is similarly modern, although there is an old quarter not too far away, where probably the building most worthy of a visit is the Église St-Jacques. Perros-Guirec represents the start of the Pink Granite coast and this church shows off the stone at its very best.

Some 8km out to sea from Perros-Guirec lies the Archipelago of the Sept Îles (and whoever counted them, there are certainly more than seven). A breeding ground for puffins and gannets, these islands are one of Brittany's most important bird reserves. Boat trips from the jetty beside the Plage de Trestraou rarely land, but simply circle the islands, allowing visitors a glimpse of these shy birds through binoculars.

26/4 On far side of marina, keep **R** to pass museum and **CA** along back of sandy beach (Plage des Arcades) • When road begins to climb, take first **R** (signed Plage de Trestignel) and ignoring waymarks, **CA** to top of hill

26/5 Turn **R** here on Rue du Pré de Saint Maur • Bear **R** on Rue de Costennou, **CA** on splendid path around Pointe du Château • At road

Pointe du Château

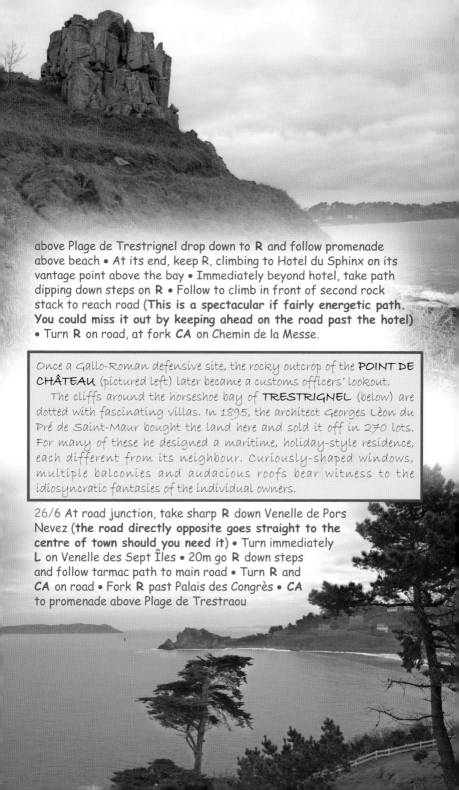

above Plage de Trestrignel drop down to **R** and follow promenade above beach • At its end, keep **R**, climbing to Hotel du Sphinx on its vantage point above the bay • Immediately beyond hotel, take path dipping down steps on **R** • Follow to climb in front of second rock stack to reach road (**This is a spectacular if fairly energetic path. You could miss it out by keeping ahead on the road past the hotel**) • Turn **R** on road, at fork **CA** on Chemin de la Messe.

Once a Gallo-Roman defensive site, the rocky outcrop of the **POINT DE CHÂTEAU** (pictured left) later became a customs officers' lookout.

The cliffs around the horseshoe bay of **TRESTRIGNEL** (below) are dotted with fascinating villas. In 1895, the architect Georges Lèon du Pré de Saint-Maur bought the land here and sold it off in 270 lots. For many of these he designed a maritime, holiday-style residence, each different from its neighbour. Curiously-shaped windows, multiple balconies and audacious roofs bear witness to the idiosyncratic fantasies of the individual owners.

26/6 At road junction, take sharp **R** down Venelle de Pors Nevez (**the road directly opposite goes straight to the centre of town should you need it**) • Turn immediately **L** on Venelle des Sept Îles • 20m go **R** down steps and follow tarmac path to main road • Turn **R** and **CA** on road • Fork **R** past Palais des Congrès • **CA** to promenade above Plage de Trestraou

9. PRACTICAL INFORMATION

SHOPS & SERVICES

- **Plougrescant** TO 02 96 92 56 83 www.ot-cotedesajoncs.com
  Mkt Sun (summer only)
- **Penvénan** TO 02 96 92 81 09 Mkt Sat
- **Perros-Guirec** TO 02 96 23 21 15 www.perros-guirec.com Mkt Fri
- Port Blanc mkt Thurs (summer only) • Louannec

ACCOMMODATION

Hotels

1. Maison Familiale des Vacances (on route) Le Coadou, Pors Scaff
   02 96 92 51 28 www.maison-familiale.ch
2. Rand'Hôtel Les Sternes (300m) Rond Point de Perros, 22700 Perros-
   Guirec 02 96 91 03 08 www.hotel-sternes-perros.com

Chambres d'hôte

3. M. Henry (200m) 22 rue des Ajoncs d'Or, Buguélès, 22710 Penvenan
   02 96 92 82 76 http://pagesperso-orange.fr/henry.location

Camping

4. Camping le Varlen (700m) 4, Route de Pors Hir, 22820 Plougrescant
   02 96 92 52 15 www.levarlen.com Open March to mid-November
5. Camping Les Dunes (on route) Port Blanc, 22710 Penvénan
   02 96 92 63 42 Open mid-June to mid-September
6. Camping Le Mat (on Route) Trestel Plage, 22600 Trévou-Tréguignec
   02 96 23 71 52 www.campinglemat.com   Open April to October
7. Camping Port l'Épine (on route) 10 Venelle Pors gor, 22660 Trélevern
   02 96 23 71 94 www.camping-port-lepine.com Open April - Sept
8. Camping Municipal Ernest Renan (on route) 66 Route de Perros, 22700
   Louannec 02 96 23 11 78 Open April to September
9. Camping Trestraou (200m) 89 Avenue du Casino, 22700 Perros-Guirec
   06 08 99 03 93 www.trestraou-camping.com Open May to September

TRANSPORT

Bus services: Port Blanc-Louannec twice daily Route 16 www.tibus.fr

Taxi: Taxi Petretti 02 96 23 20 35 Perros-Guirec

Frenet Yves 06 08 28 84 56 Perros-Guirec

Taxi Beauverger 02 96 92 63 60 Penvénan

OTHER WALKS

Plougrescant is a good starting point for circular walks taking in sections of the coast. (Free leaflet available from TO in Plougrescant)

10. Perros-Guirec - Lannion
The Pink Granite Coast
56 kms

Much of Brittany's present coastal path has its origins in the days when these shores were prowled by customs officers, but this section begins with THE Customs Officers' Path, the famous Sentier des Douaniers between Perros-Guirec and Ploumanac'h. This is now the Pink Granite Coast, and these dusky-red rocks have been weathered by wind and rain into seascapes that at times are almost surreal. Rounded, twisted, fissured, and sometimes astonishingly balanced, many of the resulting formations have been given names - the Foot, the Chameleon, Napoleon's Hat, the Sea Turtle among others. The well-trodden path ends in the beautiful rock-strewn bay of Ploumanac'h, but the curious rocky aberrations continue all the way to Trébeurden, where a benign profile entitled le Père looks out to sea. And behind this coastal scene is yet more fascination - the area is rich in megaliths with some particularly fine gallery graves.

The latter part of this section, beyond Trébeurden, presents an entirely different scene. Here the path weaves its way up and down high cliffs to the mouth of the Léguer. The steep escarpments continue right up the estuary into Lannion, but the path takes a dramatic plunge, and the last few kilometres are a more-than-comfortable stroll along the former towpath beside the river.

DIRECTIONS

27/1 Leave Plage de Trestraou on road climbing **R** • At left bend bear **R** on signed Sentier des Douaniers • **Views of the Sept Îles out to sea and the distant stacks of pink granite rock** • At forks keep **R** and **CA** 2kms to Pors Rolland • **Here the spectacle begins with the heaped up boulders of The Castle. As well as the many bizarre rock features, the path passes a Customs Officers' hut and nearby powder store as it continues towards Pors Kamor.**

PORS KAMOR

This circular cove represents the end of a one-time river valley, draining to sea. The entrance to the cove is very deep (35m), making it attractive to divers. Nearby is the lifeboat station, and beyond it, the Maison du Littoral, offering changing exhibitions on the geology and natural history of this coast. Above them, the tall pink finger of the lighthouse faces the chaotic scene to sea.

Plage St-Guirec, Ploumanac'h

• **CA** beyond Pors Kamor, past many more rocky exhibitions before turning inward around horseshoe bay of Plage St-Guirec

PLOUMANAC'H

St Guirec was a Welsh monk who landed here in the 6th century. Behind the beach is his chapel, and on the sand nearby stands an oratory containing an effigy of the saint. Legend has it that in addition to his healing skills, St-Guirec was also something of a marriage guidance counsellor. Any girl wishing to marry within the year has only to stick a pin in the saint's nose! The first statue here was in wood, and its face became so quickly disfigured that the parish decided to replace it with one of granite. Even so – well, look and see!

At the entrance to Ploumanac'h bay is an island where the turrets of a bright pink castle peep out over the pine trees. The Château de Costaérès was built in the 1890s for Polish engineer Bruno Abdank – its finest hour seems to have been when his guest Henryk Sienkiewicz completed the writing of *Quo Vadis* here.

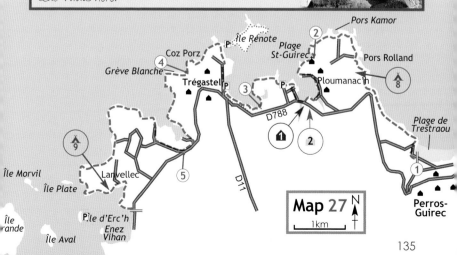

135

Tide mill, Ploumanac'h

27/2 Cross back of beach to steps in front of chapel • Bear **R** on path around headland, passing through huge stacks of rocks, to road beside harbour at Ploumanac'h • Follow road 600m beside harbour, then turn **R** to cross dyke with tide mill • Bear **R** around shore to main road • Bear **R** on road along another dyke with tide mill across estuary of Traouïero

VALLÉE DES TRAOUÏERO

Traouïero is an old Breton word meaning valleys so this is the Valley of valleys! It certainly is quite spectacular, with huge granite boulders beside – and above- the path. A footpath of about 3km in length runs through the valley and can be accessed from the first road on the left after the second tide mill (among other places). Leaflets can be obtained from local Tourist Information.

• Across second dyke, take first **R** beside port • **CA** on rough road, which bears **L** to meet the main road again. Turn **R** and keep ahead to **P** at very end • Bear **L** to coastal path and **CA** around headland, passing lake on **L**

Harbour, Ploumanac'h

PL 523000

Rocks on Île Renote

27/3 ALTERNATIVES: At **low tide**, turn **R** and walk along shore to 🅿 beside road before Trégastel • At **high tide**, **CA** to main road, turn **R**, and **R** again just before speciality shop La Trinitaine to arrive at the same point • From 🅿, **CA** up main road • At left bend, take track across rough field on **R** • Follow **L** to shore and **CA** to large 🅿 beside causeway to Île Renote

ÎLE RENOTE

A footpath runs all the way around the coast of the Île Renote, a total distance of about 2km. From the east side of the island there are splendid views of the bay of Ploumanac'h and the Château de Costaérès, and the north side has more interesting rock formations. One of these rocky stacks, accessible only at low tide, conceals a huge chasm known as le Gouffre.

• **CA** on obvious path **weaving between rocks and passing little bays of orange sand** to seafront of Coz Porz

TRÉGASTEL To the left here is the aquarium, and above it the curious white statue of Le Père Éternel (Eternal Father) on top of the rocks. He enjoys a splendid view over the reefs and rocks, which you can share by climbing steps near the aquarium exit. From the jetty at Coz Porz boat trips leave for the islands, while beneath your feet is a fine swimming pool looking directly out to sea.

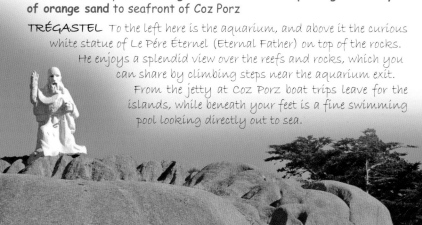

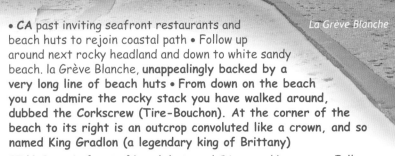

La Grève Blanche

• **CA** past inviting seafront restaurants and beach huts to rejoin coastal path • Follow up around next rocky headland and down to white sandy beach. la Grève Blanche, **unappealingly backed by a very long line of beach huts • From down on the beach you can admire the rocky stack you have walked around, dubbed the Corkscrew (Tire-Bouchon). At the corner of the beach to its right is an outcrop convoluted like a crown, and so named King Gradlon (a legendary king of Brittany)**

27/4 Cross in front of beach huts and **CA** around **L** corner • Follow path along the sea wall • **CA** over rocks to grassy area with seats above beach • Cross this directly (**maybe go down on the beach to bypass first gully**) and bear **L** to hedged path • Follow above shores of long inlet • At road, go **L** to the main road (ignore signs) • Turn **R** and follow beside busy road 300m

27/5 Take first road **R** • 500m bear **R** on Route du Grannec • At end **CA** on track • Bear **R** at fork and **CA** on **lovely stretch of coastal path** around headland • At road, **CA** past camp site • 200m bear **R** to rejoin coast path • (**There are now wonderful views of the islands as you round the Pointe de Landrellec. Nearest is the low-lying Île Plate - Flat Island - while beyond it is the not much more lofty Île Morvil. To the left of these two is the wooded Île Aval, said to be Avallon, the last resting place of King Arthur. The backdrop to them all is the heavily populated and much larger Île Grande**

• **CA** through P and bear **R** on coast path • At road **CA** through Camping Du Port • **CA** on path through woodland, coming out between houses • Turn **R** (bar and tabac to **L**) and cross wooden bridge to **CA** around bay to main road (D788)

THE CHRISTIANISED MENHIR OF ST-UZEC

This enormous standing stone was, like many others, regarded by zealous Christians as a representation of evil. In the 17th century its perceived powers were counteracted by topping it with a cross and engraving Christian symbols.

28/1 The D788 is very busy, particularly in summertime, and it would need a walk of about 3km along the fairly narrow grass verge to arrive at the access road to the Île Grande. What follows is an alternative, which includes a bonus visit to the Christianised menhir of St-Uzec.

• Follow D788 150m to first road on **L**, Chemin de Kerenoc Izellan
• Immediately bear **R** on track • **CA** 500m and turn **R** • At **TJ** turn **R** (here leaving waymarked route that is heading for St-Samson) • At next **TJ**, **CA** bearing **L** to track (Pont ar Waz) • 75m bear **L** downhill to cross stream beside house, then up to road again • **CA** to cross-roads in hamlet of Kerviziou • Cross straight over to Chemin de Clos-Moulong and **CA** on track 600m to end of tarmac road • Turn **R** on to another track between houses • 200m turn sharp **L** in front of white house and **CA** to road • Cross to road opposite, **CA** on track 1km to huge menhir with cross on top (see above)

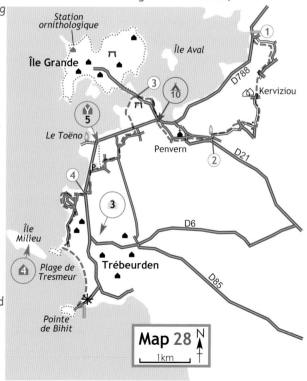

139

ÎLE GRANDE

A coastal path of about 7km encircles the Île Grande, and it is well signed, with boards showing where you are at various points. To go round anti-clockwise, once on the island take the first road on the right. Where the road bends left there is a parking area on the right giving access to the dunes at the start of the marked path.

The island is immediately different from the nearby coast in that the rock here is a blue-grey granite. On its east side, the

path gives views of the Île Aval and the bay and peninsula of Landrellec; on the north, the rocks and reefs stretch out to the

Île Aval

bare hump of le Corbeau. From this north side a path climbs up to the highest point of the island (39m) and the nearby well-preserved Allée Couverte (Gallery Grave).

On the bleak north-west corner of the island is the Station Ornithologique, an imaginative bird life information centre, with direct video links to the breeding grounds of the Sept Îles. It also functions as a bird hospital, and has done heroic work in

Station Ornithologique

the treatment of seabirds caught in oil-slicks. Beyond the Station Ornithologique the path visits the port of St-Sauveur before returning along the more tranquil bays of the south coast.

Allée couverte

28/2 Bear **R** on road, and just before main road, take narrow lane **L** • Cross over D21 to road directly opposite, soon passing Chapel of Penvern, with fontaine outside • *CA* 120m, turn **R** • *CA* to main road (D788) • Cross diagonally to continue on D21 • 250m take rough road serving houses on **R** • At end *CA* on open grassy area above shore • Turn **L** between stone walls to return to road

DIVERSION: cross causeway and circumnavigate Île Grande

28/3 (**DIVERSION: A few metres down the road at this point is another impressive Allée Couverte - pictured above - well worth the diversion. The track leading to it is marked. Return to point** 28/3)
MAIN ROUTE: take track almost opposite gap in stone wall • *CA* 300m then follow **L** (tracks to **R** lead to menhir on the shore) • *CA* on widest track to return to D788 • Cross to road opposite and *CA* 250m to cross-roads • Turn **R** • At **TJ** go **L** • 200m take road on **R** • Where this road swings right, *CA* descending steeply • At bottom, turn **R**
DIVERSION: After a few metres, a track on the R leads to the Youth Hostel near the main road. From there, on the opposite side of the D788, a rough road out across the marsh passes a menhir known as Le Toëno

Le Toëno

Trébeurden

• **CA** on road to ℗ beside D788 • Turn **L** on main road • 150m take road on **L** running beside Marais du Quellen • Follow back to main road

THE MARAIS DU QUELLEN This freshwater marsh is a haven for wildlife. White Camargue horses who feel at home in this environment have been imported to keep the vegetation under control.

28/4 At D788 again, cross diagonally **L** to road opposite • Follow **L**, then turn **R** on Rue du Roc'h ar Skoed • **CA** on Allée Circulaire de Lan Kerellec • Follow **L** to **TJ**, turn **R** to junction, turn **R** and bear **R** to descend to harbour, **with glorious views of Trébeurden, its port and its islands ahead.**

TRÉBEURDEN

A modern marina protected by a long wall of granite boulders sits beneath the strange pink granite outcrop known as Le Castel. It is well worth taking the 15 minute walk around this for yet another exhibition of elements-induced rock sculpture. On the south side the deeply wrinkled face on the cliff has been dubbed le Père - the Father of Trébeurden. The île Milliau is less easily accessed, but should the water be low enough, paths on the island lead up to an allée couverte in a splendid location. Other islands can be seen off Trébeurden, low reefs like Molène and Losquet that you feel might almost disappear under the waves. Boat trips take curious visitors out in summertime.

Rocks on Le Castel

Île Milliau *and Le Castel*

• **CA** past port and access to Le Castel • Follow promenade behind Plage de Tresmeur, **a popular family beach** • At its far end, **CA** on coastal path climbing to round Pointe de Bihit

• At road **ALTERNATIVES**: **either** turn **R** and walk round the point, **or** walk **L** up road to toposcope (splendid view of Trébeurden from here, **or** cross road and bear **L** on path to continue along coast

29/1 (see p.145) **CA** on coastal path to road above beach of Pors Mabo • Cross this to Chemin du Can opposite and go **R** • 400m, then double back **R** (signed Camping du Kerdual) • Past campsite's entrance, **CA** on track along cliff 2km to arrive at Vallée de Goas Lagorn • **This beautiful little valley has been managed as a conservation site since 1978** • **CA** behind fine sandy beach, cross **P** and pass in front of crêperie (summertime only) and little Auberge de Jeunesse • Rejoin coastal path • Follow to top of cliff, passing below lighthouse

Lighthouse of Beg Léguer, Pointe de Servel

Vallée de Goas Lagorn

Estuary of River Léguer

- Immediately past this (before tarmac), take track **R** • Follow down to cross back of another beach • **CA** past blockhaus on Pointe Servel

29/2 Around point, climb and bear **L** to **P** • Bear **R** to regain coastal path • **CA with some panoramic views of the estuary and the Baie de la Vierge opposite** • At turning area in front of houses, go **L** on road, then, **beside a fine calvary**, **R** on path behind house • Descend steeply to road running alongside estuary and turn **L** • At left bend away from estuary, **CA** on towpath beside river • Follow 5.5kms to bridge in Lannion, **Pont de Viarmes**

Calvaire Beg Hent

Towpath along the Leguer

LANNION

The coastal path crosses the bridge so avoiding the town, but those who want to visit it can keep straight ahead until past the Tourist Information Office, then bear left to the centre.

In the Middle Ages, Lannion was a flourishing port trading in fabrics, silk and cereals. The wealthy merchants of the time left their legacy to the town in an array of fine half-timbered or slate-fronted houses, gathered around the Place du Général Leclerc and in the narrow streets nearby. This handsome centre is well worth the short diversion. Other buildings of note are the two churches. The Église St-Jean-du-Baly is a 16th century edifice tucked into the old town, but the Église de Brélévenez, founded much earlier by the Knights Templar, enjoys a far more exalted position. Perched on a hill above the town, a mere 142 steps are required to reach it and appreciate its view across the houses to the valley of the Léguer. Interior features of note are a stoup once used for measuring wheat brought in tithe, and a Romanesque crypt rather spookily concealed beneath the chancel.

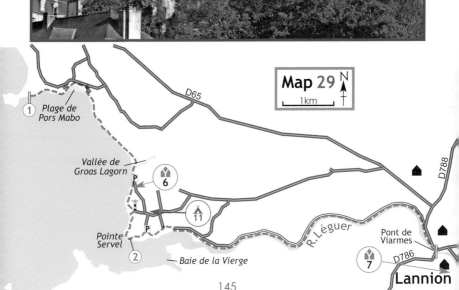

10. PRACTICAL INFORMATION

SHOPS & SERVICES

- **Perros-Guirec** TO 02 96 23 21 15 www.perros-guirec.com Mkt Fri
- **Trébeurden** TO 02 96 23 51 64 www.trebeurden.fr Mkt Tues
- **Lannion** TO 02 96 46 41 00 www.ot-lannion.fr Mkt Thurs
- **Ploumanac'h** • **Trégastel** • **Île Grande**

ACCOMMODATION

Hotels

1. Hotel Albatros (on route) 81 Bd des Traouïeros, Ploumanac'h, 22700 Perros-Guirec 02 96 91 42 04 hotel.albatros@wanadoo.fr

Chambres d'hôte

2. Mme Coatanhay (200m) 61 boulevard des Traouïeros, Ploumanac'h, 22700 Perros-Guirec 02 96 91 66 61 angelcoat@wanadoo.fr au61.free.fr Open all year
3. Mme le Guillouzic (400m) 19bis rue de Kerwenet, 22560 Trébeurden 02 96 23 59 01 almanzaref@orange.fr

Gite d'étape

4. Île Milliau (access at low tide) Trébeurden (TO) 02 96 23 51 64

Auberge de Jeunesse

5. Le Toëno (on diversion to Le Toëno) 60 Route de la Corniche, 22560 Trébeurden 02 96 23 52 22 Open March - September
6. Beg Léguer (on route) Plage de Goas Lagorn, Beg Leguer, 22300 Lannion 02 96 47 24 86 Open mid April - mid September
7. Les Korrigans (500m) Rive Gauche, 6, Rue du 73ième Terminal, 22300 Lannion 02 96 37 91 28 Open all year

Camping

8. Camping le Ranolien (300m) Pors Rolland, Ploumanac'h, 22700 Perros-Guirec 02 96 91 65 65 www.leranolien.fr Open April to mid-Sept
9. Camping du Port (on route) Landrellec, 22560 Pleumeur-Bodou 02 96 23 87 79 www.camping-du-port.com Open late March to early October
10. Camping l'Espérance (on route), Rue de Keralegan, Penvern, 22560 Trébeurden 02 96 91 95 05 www.camping-esperance.com Open April to September
11. Camping les Plages de Beg Léguer (300m), Route de la Côte, 22300, Lannion 02 96 47 27 77 Open Easter to early November

TRANSPORT

Bus services: Tibus route 15 Lannion - Perrso-Guirec - Ploumanac'h - Trégastel - Trébeurden - Lannion (both directions) www.tibus.fr

Taxi: Le Vot, Bernard 02 96 23 55 05 / 06 71 04 56 11 Trébeurden
Allo Armor Taxi 06 11 07 09 86 Lannion

OTHER WALKS

The Vallée des Traouïeros, the Marais du Quellen and the Vallée de Goas Lagorn all offer walks of around an hour in duration. The Île Grande and the Île Renote can both be explored on circular coastal paths.

11. Lannion - Locquirec

Baie de Lannion

35 kms

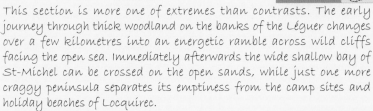

This section is more one of extremes than contrasts. The early journey through thick woodland on the banks of the Léguer changes over a few kilometres into an energetic ramble across wild cliffs facing the open sea. Immediately afterwards the wide shallow bay of St-Michel can be crossed on the open sands, while just one more craggy peninsula separates its emptiness from the camp sites and holiday beaches of Locquirec.

Archaeologists have two particular treats in this section. The first of these is the site of le Yaudet on a peninsula at the mouth of the Léguer, where excavations have revealed evidence of Neolithic and Roman occupation. The second is the well-preserved remains of a Roman bath-house known as the Thermes de Hogolo, picturesquely sited above the golden sands of the Grève des Cures.

At the end of the section the path crosses the Douron estuary to leave Côtes d'Armor and enter Finistère. Locquirec, the first town, is surely a good ambassador for its department, a totally unspoilt little resort with a most attractive port area.

DIRECTIONS

30/1 Directly across Pont de Viarmes in Lannion, turn **R** • Follow minor road alongside River Léguer 2km • When road leaves river **CA** on path into dense woodland • **This is an ancient woodland of oak, beech and holly with a carpet of bluebells in springtime. Several paths wind through it, but the one to follow is always well-signed. In any case, guided by the river, although only briefly glimpsed through the foliage in summertime, you can't really go wrong. What follows here is just a brief outline of the major twists and turns.**

• Soon after entering wood, at gap in wall, turn **L** and climb, then bear **R** on broad track • At next **TJ** bear **R**, soon crossing stream on railway sleeper bridge • Pass alongside open grassy area • At fork by signpost bear **R** downhill towards estuary • Cross stream on wooden bridge, climb to meet broader track and bear **R** • **Beyond a beach with a gaunt skeleton of an old boat, other boats moored in the estuary can be glimpsed through the trees** • Eventually houses can be seen on clifftop ahead and path reaches a junction with a broad track • Follow this **R**, descending to little quay at le Yaudet

30/2 Cross straight over and **CA** around headland • Pass two stone customs officers' huts, and beside fontaine climb steps to top of hill • Walk **L** across grass to Chapelle du Yaudet

Pointe de Dourven from Le Yaudet

LE YAUDET

Le Yaudet is sited on a high-cliffed granite promontory, obviously ideally placed to mount a guard on the estuary of the Léguer. Limited excavation of the site had been carried out previously, but between 1991 and 2002 it was the subject of investigation by a joint team from the University of Oxford and the Université de Bretagne Occidentale. They found that the site had been in almost continuous occupation for some 8000 years. The ramparts that can still be seen on the landward side were additions in the late Iron Age. The Romans occupied the site under the name of Vetus Civitas, and built a wall on the sea side to defend it from marauding Saxons and Vikings. The latter burnt the place down in 836 AD. There is some suggestion that Le Yaudet was the seat of the first Breton bishopric – and more imaginative minds have it that it was the site of Asterix's Gallic village. Sadly for such a colourful history, there is little other than the ramparts and a few stones of the Roman wall to see today.

The chapel was built as recently as 1860, but it stands on the site of a very much older establishment, and that in its turn was built over a Roman temple. Inside the chapel is an altarpiece with a rare depiction of the Mother and Child lying in bed.

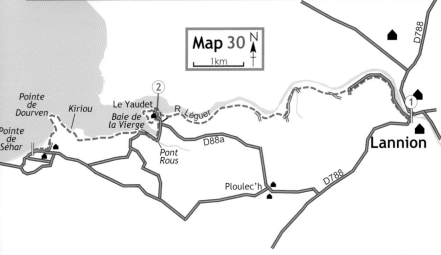

149

Plage de Kiriou

• From chapel go down to road (ignore signed path), turn **R** • At junction bear **R** (signed Locquémeau) • Follow down to cross Pont Rous, then follow **R** uphill.

PONT ROUS stands at the head of the Baie de la Vierge. At low tide an arc of stones can be seen blocking off the bay. The structure dates from Medieval times, and is thought to have been a fish trap or the dyke of a tide mill.

• 250m take broad gravelled track on **R** • Follow beside bay and enter woodland • Beyond gates of a property, descend to idyllic cove of Kiriou • **CA** behind sandy beach towards Pointe de Dourven • Ignore steps on **L** and **CA** (**The steps lead to a Centre of Contemporary Art on the Point. It can also be reached from the tip by climbing past the customs officers' hut, beside which there are a few rather worn sculptures**) • **CA** around headland, passing a curious ensemble of rocks at the tip, from where there is a fine view of the Pointe de Séhar across the bay

View of Pointe de Séhar from the Pointe de Dourven

Leaving Locquémeau and the Pointe de Séhar

• **CA** alongside field, then between hedges and fences to rough road serving houses • **CA** to larger road, turn **R** and walk down to seafront at Locquémeau

---

LOCQUÉMEAU

Locquémeau occupies a sheltered position between the rocky Pointe de Dourven and the long flat spit of the Pointe de Séhar. Once a centre of sardine fishing, now only a handful of boats remain in its harbour and they are more concerned with mackerel or shellfish. Today Locquémeau is developing its tourist potential, although with its rocky beach and offshore reefs, it is not an obvious holiday destination.

31/1 (see map p.) **CA** behind bay, keeping **R** on road to reach town centre • Turn **R** on main road towards Pointe de Séhar • Just before point, turn sharp **L** on rough road • Past house, **CA** on coastal path

THE CLIFFS OF TRÉDREZ At this point you are embarking on a cliff path that extends for 6.5kms to St-Michel-en-Grève. The first part of the route presents no particular difficulties, but after the signed junction at 31/2 where the Gr34B heads off inland up the cliffs, the path steps up a gear, becoming generally more exposed and incorporating a few rocky scrambles. Anyone with a tendency to vertigo would have problems with the final headland, Beg ar Forn, but beyond it, all is well again, with an easy amble into St-Michel.

ALTERNATIVE: Should you wish to avoid the cliff path, it is easy to get to the same point using roads and tracks on the plateau above (see map 31)

Cliffs of Trédrez

Approaching St-Michel-en-Grève

31/2 CA 2kms to headland of Beg ar Forn • After headland bear **R** to continue along coast • Descend to beach and cross it to slipway beside church • Bear **R** at road and bear **R** ahead at main road through Saint-Michel-en-Grève

ST MICHEL-EN-GRÈVE AND ITS BAY

St Michel stands at the corner of the Lieue de Grève, a shallow horseshoe bay in which the sea retreats some 2km at low tide. The perfect curve of the bay is disrupted in the centre by an 84m high cliff known as the Grand Rocher. In medieval times, this wooded outcrop was the haunt of brigands and highwaymen who preyed on pilgrims and other travellers going between St Efflam and St Michel. At high tide, the passage beside the rock was very narrow and served as a trap, while at low tide they could walk out less fearfully on the sands. A cross (known as the Croix de Mi-Lieue) was planted in the middle of the bay to give voyagers some idea of the state of the tide and of the direction they must take for a safe passage.

Today the Lieue de Grève has another menace – pollution. Every summer sees the bay filled with green algae, which under the suns rays, develops an offensive smell. With tourism under threat, a clean-up operation is carried out throughout the summer months. The cause is reputedly the nitrates used in farming, carried down by rivers to this shallow bay and others farther west.

31/3 ALTERNATIVES: Today, with no cross, no brigands and only the algae and the tide to take into account, you can **EITHER** make your own way across the sands to point 31/4 **OR** walk on the pavement beside the road. (The signed coastal path actually takes a big detour

Grand Rocher

inland from St-Michel – follow it by all means, but it will add a distance of about 7km to the journey)

Road route: walk along grassy bank above beach for a few hundred metres to where pavement begins • **CA** 2kms to Ⓟ at foot of Grand Rocher • **From here a clear path climbs to the summit with its splendid view (see p.154)** • **CA** around bay to where main road swings away inland

31/4 Bear **R** on minor road, signed Chapelle St-Efflam

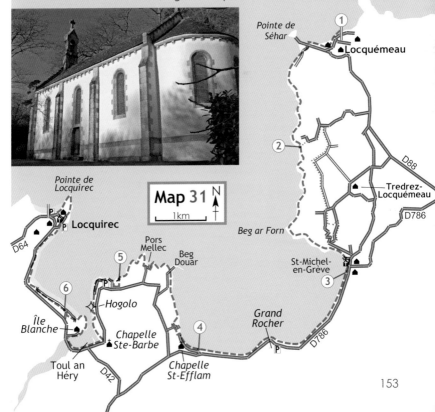

Path up the Grand Rocher

ST EFFLAM

St Efflam, the son of a king, landed here after crossing from Ireland in the 6th century. Several legends and miracles are attributed to him, but he is most often associated with the story of King Arthur and the dragon – a dragon the size of a bull, with one red eye, green scales around its shoulders and other memorable features. Apparently Arthur was pursuing the dragon along these shores when he became exhausted. St Efflam arrived on the scene, tapped his stick on a rock and brought forth a spring of fresh water that revived Arthur immediately. Whether it was actually Arthur or Efflam who then killed the dragon seems in dispute, but the evil beast certainly fell into the sea and was never seen again. St Efflam is usually depicted with a dragon at his feet as on the side of the chapel here – and the healing water still springs from the rock beneath.

• Pass fontaine and steps to chapel, and **CA** to end of road • Bear **L**, on coastal path climbing into woods • Bear **R** to continue above bay • At road follow **L** 70m, then take path **R** • At road above little harbour of Beg Douar cross straight over to **CA** on coastal path • At road leading to beach at Pors Mellec, turn **L** uphill • Follow **R**, then at left-hand bend, **CA** and bear **R** on coastal path • **A section employing many log steps follows, after which the path becomes easier, with views across to Locquirec**

31/5 At fork in path, go **L** uphill to come out between stone houses on road • Turn **R** on road • 250m take track on **R** • At P take road ahead, parallel to beach • At end bear **L** off road to **CA** on path under pine trees • Follow to site of Gallo-Roman bathhouse

Beg Douar

LES THERMES DU HOGOLO

Discovered in 1982, these baths date back to the first century AD. The waters were heated by fires below the ground, and bathers progressed from baths of tepid water through the steam room to finish in the cold bath. A display board (with English translation) points out the various features.

• Leaving Baths, take middle of three paths • Go round wooden barrier and **CA** on path below road • Follow along edge of inlet and **CA** 600m to road beside harbour of Toul an Héry • **Just to the left here the early 17th century Chapelle Ste-Barbe hides itself among the stone houses**

• Turn **R** on road and follow around port and across long bridge over the Douron **now entering département of Finistère** • Over bridge take first road on **R** • At gates of rather grand property of Île Blanche, go down to beach • **CA** along back of beach (climbing up into the grounds of Île Blanche is permitted only at highest of tides) • **CA** on raised path • Facing bay, keep behind wooden palisade to meet road

Estuary of R.Douron at Toul an Héry

Locquirec

31/6 Cross to path continuing along bank under pine trees • At road again, turn **R**, and before beach, turn **L** along main track through large campsite • At far side, cross road leading to beach and **CA** into another camping area • Bear **L** around first building to gap in hedge leading to broad track • Turn **R** and at main road, **R** again • **CA** on road • Finally bear **R** to descend to port at Locquirec

LOCQUIREC

Locquirec takes its name from St Guirec, a Welsh monk of the 6th century, who was sent by St Tugdual to evangelise this area. Its livelihood once depended on the harvest of the sea, but although there are still fishing boats in the harbour, tourism has taken over. Locquirec has nine different beaches to offer the holidaymaker, but its real charm lies in its lack of sophistication or commercialism.

• From port **CA** past church • At left corner, bear **R** • At end of road **CA** on gravelled path • **CA** around Pointe de Locquirec to meet main road (D64) beside sweeping sands of Pors-ar-Villiec • Pass through P to **CA** up main road

11. PRACTICAL INFORMATION

SHOPS & SERVICES
- Locquémeau
- St-Michel-en-Grève TO 02 96 35 74 87 (school holidays only)
- Plestin-Les-Grèves (2.5kms) TO 02 96 35 61 93
  www.officetourisme-delalieuedegreve.com
- Locquirec TO 02 98 67 40 83 www.locquirec.com Mkt Wed

ACCOMMODATION
Rand'Hôtel

1. Rand'Hôtel de la Baie (on route) 22, Rue du Port, 22300 Locquémeau
   02 96 35 23 11 www.hotel-delabaie.com
2. Les Panoramas (on route) 9 rue Poul Guioc'h, Pte de Beg Douar,
   Plestin-les-Grèves 02 96 35 63 76 hotel.les.panoramas@wanadoo. fr
   http://lespanoramas.ifrance.com

Chambres d'hôte

3. M&Mme Le Cunff (300m) Kerham-Uhellan, 22300 Tredrez-Locquémeau
   02 96 35 21 34 martine.daniel.le-cunff@wanadoo.fr www.chambres-
   tregor.com/locquemeau
4. Kervellec (200m) 11 rue de Pors ar Viellec, 29241 Locquirec
   02 98 67 45 24 Open all year

Camping

5. Camping Municipal St Efflam (on route) Rue de Lan-Carré, 22310
   Plestin-les-Grèves 02 96 35 62 15 Open April to September
6. Camping Municipal les Pins (on route) Route de Plestin, 29241
   Locquirec 02 98 67 45 79 or Mairie 02 98 67 42 20 Open April - Sept

TRANSPORT

Bus services: Tibus route 30 Lannion - Morlaix stops at St Michel-en-
Grève, St Efflam, Toul an Héry and Locquirec. About 5 buses a day in
each direction, but check timetable www.tibus.fr

Taxi: Taxi Plestinais 02 96 35 69 50 Plestin-les-Grèves
   Taxi Nanou 06 10 28 89 89 Locquirec
   Taxi Quéré 02 98 67 40 00 Locquirec

OTHER WALKS

The peninsula between the estuary of the Douron and the Grève
St-Michel can be negotiated as a circular walk of 9 km. From near the
Chapelle Ste-Barbe a footpath heads uphill beside the stream, reaching
the hamlet of Trou an Dour, from where the circuit an be completed to
St-Efflam by road. (IGN map 0615ET will help)

Those who are comfortable with cliff-walking can use the main route and
the alternative to make a circuit on the plateau of Tredrez-Locquémeau
(see map 31).

The Tourist Office at Locquirec can offer a free leaflet of 7 walks in the
area.

12. Locquirec - Morlaix

Bas Trégor

46 kms

The first part of this section is more remote and wild than anything encountered so far. In 9km of path winding along the exposed north-facing cliff, the only hint of civilisation is a couple of picnic tables situated behind the tiny cove of Vilin Izella. The sea pounds the rocks at the foot of the cliffs and seaward there is nothing to see other than the odd coastal fishing boat that passes this way. The Pointe de Primel and the Pointe du Diben, both well-inhabited, herald the change. The path turns south again, along the gentle shores of the Bay of Morlaix, and the view is of a thousand scattered islands, and distant Roscoff and the Île de Batz. On its own peninsula, the enormous prehistoric burial chamber known as the Cairn of Barnenez is more than worth a visit, after which Dourduff-en-Mer offers the last delightful views of this coast before the path heads inland to Morlaix.

Plage de Porz Villiec

DIRECTIONS

32/1 Follow D64 climbing away from Plage de Pors ar Villiec • Half-way up hill (at end of line of houses), take track **R** downhill • At narrow road, turn **L** (uphill again), then bear **R** beside Fontaine de Saint Kiriec • Keep **R** on path to go round Pointe du Corbeau • **CA** to emerge between properties above beach of Les Sables Blancs • Cross long grassy area to P • From its lowest level, descend log steps to sunken lane behind beach • Follow through scrubland on cliff, **CA** around headland and descend to road at Moulin de la Rive • Turn **R** past P, and just beyond it, take minor road on **R** (signed St-Jean-du-Doigt) • 150m (opposite road junction) take coastal path down on **R** • Follow around cliff at lower level • **The cliff path here is not too demanding, but if preferred, continue on the road. At its highest point, a *table d'orientation* that has seen better days can still identify some of the features of this wild seascape**

32/2 Climb to road and turn **R** • **CA** to **TJ** at Poul Rodou, **where there is a restaurant and a curious café-cum-bookshop** • To R of this, **CA** on coastal path (**At Poul Rodou, a sign on the coastal path states that it is taken at your own risk. In truth it is perhaps only a little more ambitious than the previous section of cliff path, but it is certainly as well to take extra care**)

Vilin Izella

Moulin de Trobodec

• **CA** 2kms to 🅿 above tiny beach at Vilin Izella (sometimes also called Vénizella) • **The picnic area beside the car park has a memorial to the Resistance, who once operated from these lonely shores**

DIVERSION: 200m up the road here is the Moulin de Trobodec, a restored functional watermill with an enormous wheel. The mill is open to visitors in summertime. Far from home, two Highland cattle graze in the fields alongside

32/3 Walk through picnic area to turn **L** up steps at its end • Follow coast path around and up to summit of Beg an Fry, where there is a path junction

Map 32

1km

Approaching St-Jean-du-Doigt

ALTERNATIVE: Once again there are warnings on this cliff path, and this indeed is one to respect. The precipitous drop from the heights of Beg an Fry is followed by a very undulating section with one or two rocky scrambles added. This sort of drama lasts only for the first 3km or so. The remainder (of similar length) is tame by comparison – although the sting-in-the-tail is a couple of sharp ascents.

To take the cliff path, turn **R** on summit of Beg an Fry (signed Pointe de Runglaz) and drop steeply downhill • *CA* around Pointe Runglaz.

If tackling the cliff path does not appeal, turn **L** at the path junction on Beg an Fry, follow through to the road at Prajou and turn **R** (or leave out Beg an Fry and walk up the road from the mill). Then follow the road through to St-Jean-du-Doigt, turning **R** to return to the coast

33/1 **At a fork in the path here it is posible to join a track, then to follow the road to Plage de St-Jean-du-Doigt, thereby avoiding the 'sting-in-the-tail' climbs on the cliff path. There is another opportunity to join the road about 600m from the end of the path**

• Where cliff path ends at road, turn **R** to walk downhill • *CA* past Plage de St-Jean-du-Doigt (restaurants)

DIVERSION: The little town of St-Jean-du-Doigt is 1km to the left here by the road (D79): return same route

ST JEAN-DU-DOIGT

Its name derives from its most prized possession – the first joint of the index finger of St-John the Baptist, held in the church treasury. The relic has always been associated with the healing of eye complaints, and when Anne of Brittany herself benefited from its powers (c1500), she gave generously towards the building of the church. It has a fine triumphal arch, an oratory with an interestingly-shaped roof and an impressive fountain on which God the Father presides over Christ's baptism by St-John.

33/2 Follow road climbing away from beach • With church of
Plougasnou ahead, double back **R** on tarmac path flanked by railings
• Bear **R** again to pass Chapel of Ker Maria • **CA** alongside its wall
• Follow path down, passing lavoir as it levels out • **CA** on this up and
down path to fork • **The path ahead goes on to skirt the coast but
at the present time (Spring 2008) it is not open to the public.
Should the situation be different in the future, this will definitely
be the quickest way to reach Primel-Trégastel** • For the present,
turn **L** at fork, and climb inland • At farmhouse turn **R** • At lane, go **L**
to meet road • Turn **R** on road, passing through cultivated fields
• Bear **R** at fork (Route de Rhun Izella) to reach seafront at Primel-
Trégastel (**The town of Primel-Trégastel sits astride the base of a
long promontory – The Pointe de Primel. With beaches facing both
east and west it has holiday appeal, and recent years have seen a
regeneration of interest with the creation of a new sea wall and
various building projects**)

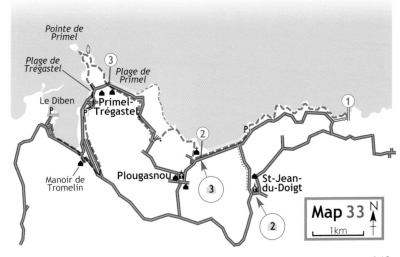

Pointe de Primel

33/3 From far end of promenade go down on to beach, leaving it by obvious steps ahead • Follow path skirting houses on cliff, then campsite, to reach Pointe de Primel

---

POINTE DE PRIMEL

Anyone in a hurry could easily bypass this promontory, but it well repays exploration. Situated at the entrance to the Bay of Morlaix it has been used as a guard post for a very long time - the ramparts at its base date back to the Mesolithic period, 8,000 to 6,000 BC. The Cabane des Douaniers on the summit belongs to the 18th century when Customs Officers patrolled this coast, but even in the last World War this was used as a lookout post.

The rock of the point is a brownish-red fine-grained granite, as is well shown in the menhir on the eastern side. This handsome stone (the one on the cover of this book) was 'discovered' in the clean-up after the Amoco-Cadiz catastrophe (1978), and re-erected.

The farthest tip is cut off from the rest of the Point by the Gouffre, a narrow abyss some 12m deep. With water swirling in its depths at high tide, at low tide it is dry and it is just possible to attempt a crossing.

• **CA** on road skirting Plage de Trégastel and bear **R** on main road • 100m turn **L** on Rue de Kereven • **CA** on Chemin de Parc ar Born • **CA** on Chemin de la Carrière to meet main road at **P** • Turn **L**, taking raised tarmac path to **L** of road • **CA** where this becomes tarmac road • 500m turn **R** to cross main road, doubling back **R** • **CA** to take Chemin de Tromelin **L**, dipping into valley and bearing **L** • In front of Manoir de Tromelin, turn **R** to meet main road • Turn **L** on main road • At end of harbour, take first **R** and almost immediately turn **L** • **CA**, then turn **R** to reach seafood premises at port of le Diben

Manoir de Tromelin

LE DIBEN

Le Diben is an attractive fishing village, but its port areas are today dominated by the premises of a major shellfish enterprise. The *viviers* are the 'fishponds', the tanks where crabs, lobsters and the like are held before being sold fresh. It is possible to take a tour at certain times.

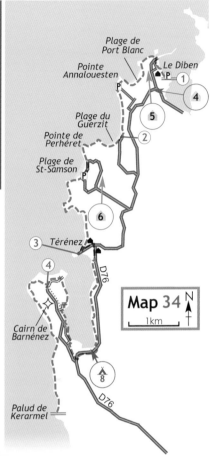

34/1 From **P** beside port take path on **L**, skirting beach and continuing as alleyway between houses • Coming out between second stone gateposts, turn **R** on road (**above premises of Les Viviers du Diben**) • At main road to port turn **R**, then **L** onto heathland opposite • Follow path running past first huge stack of red rock, then bearing **L** to pass in front of houses around Plage de Port Blanc • Reaching Pointe Annalouesten, bear **L** to top of hill (**R** is a risky cliffside track) and **CA** over it to **P** below

Rocks at Le Diben

POINTE ANNALOUESTEN

The remains of a Corps de Garde can be seen on the summit. There are superb views of the bay from here, and among the islands you can pick out one that seems to be all building. This is the Château du Taureau, a stronghold fashioned by Vauban to guard the Rade de Morlaix, and at the foot of the Pointe a 'sight-guide' has been installed to make sure you don't miss it.

The château you see today is obviously the work of Vauban, but it was built on the site of an earlier defence placed here after an incident in 1522. Morlaix pirates had attacked Bristol, and Henry VIII sent out the English fleet in retaliation. Fortuitously they arrived when all Morlaix's dignitaries were out feasting, and the town was quickly sacked. The victory was not all it might have been because the English decided to avail themselves of the town's wine cellars and so became easy prey. But the people of Morlaix vowed that never again would the town be taken unawares.

The Château du Taureau has in more recent times been used as a prison, as a sailing school and even as a private residence.

Le Guerzit

• From P̄ bear **R** down steps to regain coastal path, continuing along base of high cliff to arrive at beach of le Guerzit

34/2 **CA** along beach • Leave between house wall and bank of pebbles • **CA** around wooded Pointe de Perhéret to meet road to large P̄ at beach of St-Samson • **CA** along alleyway to **L** of big house • **CA** on sandy track along coast, **passing curious twisted rock formation dubbed the Pierre Double** • Follow track hugging coast around next peninsula and **CA** to the village of Térénez • **This section has splendid views of the many tiny islands that are now an ornithological reserve, and of Carantec (with the long promontory of the Ile Callot) behind them across the bay. Farther back still are Roscoff and the Île de Batz (see Walking the Brittany Coast, Vol 2)**

34/3 At port area turn sharp **L** • Follow road 250m up to junction with D76 • Turn **R** on D76 • 300m, double back **R** on track • Go down steps to follow path **L** along coast below level of road • 2km rejoin road to

Pierre Double

THE CAIRN OF BARNENEZ

With the increase of road building in the 1950s, contractors thought they had found a valuable source of stone when they quarried into the hill at Barnenez. It was only when they broke through into one of the chambers of this cairn that they had enough insight to halt operations. Archaeologists took over, and revealed a cairn containing 11 separate burial chambers, the whole standing some 75m long and 8m high. The cairn had been built in two stages – the first 5 chambers dating from around 4500BC were in local dolerite stone, while for the 'extension' some 300 years or more later, stone from the île Sterec had been transported. No bones were found in the cairn, but pottery and polished axe-heads were recovered and some of the stones in the chambers bore symbolic engravings, of which there are copies on the site today. The Cairn of Barnenez is open to visitors every day (except Mondays in winter), but the chambers have been sealed off, and the best glimpses of its interior are through the part exposed by quarrying on the north-west side.

cross bridge • **CA** on road 500m to junction • Turn **R** (signed Cairn de Barnenez) • In front of bar/crêperie take track on **R** down to estuary and follow **L** • **CA** on narrow walled lane • At road turn **R** • 250m turn **R** on track signed La Petite Grève (private premises)

DIVERSION: CA up road to visit the Cairn of Barnenez • Afterwards, either return to track signed La Petite Grève or continue up the road to pointe 34/4

• At end of track turn **L** on path behind ostreiculture premises
• Follow 500 to track, turn **L** • **CA** to junction in front of houses

34/4 Turn **R** here (the Cairn is to the left) and **CA** on scenic path descending steeply to follow coast • **CA** 2.5kms to Palud de Kerarmel

Oyster beds and the Château de Taureau

Le Palud de Kerarmel

Oyster beds fill the bay here and the port of Le Palud de Keremel is given over to the enterprise.

35/1 **At Le Palud de Kerarmel, briefly join road • At left bend CA on path 2kms to bridge at Le Dourduff-en-Mer**

LE DOURDUFF-EN-MER

Le Dourduff is a port protected by a natural cordon of pebbles. Now concerned only with coastal fishing and the oyster industry, it was once a busy commercial port and in medieval times a centre of marine craftsmanship. Anne of Brittany's famous ship La Cordelière, later lost to the English at the Battle of St-Mathieu, was built here in 1500.

• Turn R to cross over long road bridge, then immediately turn L on shady path beside River Dourduff (although very scenic, the D76 to Morlaix is not recommended for walking) • At broad gravelled track, turn R • 150m turn R beside EDF (electricity) tower • Follow path up through woods (a 'coquille' sign on a post indicates that you are on one of Brittany's ancient pilgrim routes to Santiago de Compostela) • The Château of Sucinio stands across the valley on the right

CHÂTEAU AND PARC BOTANIQUE OF SUSCINIO

The 16th century Château of Suscinio once belonged to local corsair Charles Cornic. Now an agricultural college, its gardens are carefully tended to give an all-year-round display and are open to the public every day. They include such features as the 'Garden of the Corsair', the 'Valley of the Lost Worlds' and the 'Children's Village' with its tree house.

35/2 Bear **R** to pass between college buildings and château • At crossroads **CA** • At fork, bear **L** on main road • At **TJ** go **L** • 100m go **R** to reach town of Ploujean • Bear **R** in front of church

THE CHURCH OF PLOUJEAN

is proud of its associations with Marechal Foch, Supreme Commander of the Allied Armies at the end of World War I. He owned the nearby estate of Tréfeunteuniou and came here to worship. His pew is in the chapel on the right hand side and there is a memorial to him nearby.

• At end of church wall, turn **L** on wide track passing school • **CA** on avenue of trees leading to farm of Roz ar Ménez • Follow **L** and **R** between farm buildings (**These are now the grounds of the private 19th century Château of Keranroux, and the signed path deviates to avoid the Château itself**) • After

Dovecote at Keranroux

170

farm, take track heading into woodland on **L** • At large rock, turn **R** and in a few metres, **R** again towards château • 200m bend **L** going downhill to cross track to château • **CA** into valley (**where there is a sunken monumental fountain**) • Bear **R** in front of dovecote • Follow path to ornamental gate onto road • Turn **R**, follow road under motorway viaduct • At D76 turn **L** and walk alongside river • At junction **CA** past port and on into Morlaix

MORLAIX

Morlaix's most enduring image is that of the huge viaduct striding over its old houses, tying together the halves of the town on either side of the deep river valley. Built here in the 1860s to carry the new Paris to Brest railway line, whatever must the residents of the time have thought of their new feature that is now something of an icon?

Naturally Morlaix goes back a lot farther than its viaduct. In the Middle Ages it was a thriving fishing port, also dealing in woven cloth and tobacco. Like St-Malo it became a focus for corsairs and was centre-stage in the long years of tit-for-tat battles with the English. The motto added to the coat of arms after the incident in 1522 (see p.166) says it all – S'ils te mordent, morde-les (If they bite you, bite them back). Of course it is also a clever pun on the town's name.

For those arriving on foot along the riverside, the old town lies beyond the arches of the viaduct, and cries out to be explored. Simply wandering through the ancient alleyways gives a good feel for the place, but the Tourist Office (almost beneath the viaduct) offers a more detailed tour of its museums, churches and lovely half-timbered buildings. Morlaix also boasts an assortment of interesting individual shops.

**At Morlaix this story must end – but you have only sampled a
fraction of Brittany's magnificent and addictive coastline.
The next volume in this series takes you on to Bénodet...**

12. PRACTICAL INFORMATION

SHOPS & SERVICES

- **Plougasnou** TO 02 98 67 31 88 www.tourisme-plougasnou.com
- **Morlaix** 02 98 62 14 94 www.morlaixtourisme.fr Mkt Sat

ACCOMMODATION

Hotels

1. Hotel du Port (on route) 02 98 88 07 54. Quai de Léon, 29600 Morlaix. www.lhotelduport.com

Chambres d'hôte

2. La Metairie (900m) Rue de la Duchesse Anne de Bretagne, 29630 St-Jean-du-Doigt 02 98 67 82 31 http://lametairie.aliosphere.com
3. Mme Vigor (200m) Feunteunigou, 22 route de la Plage, 29630 Plougasnou 02 98 67 82 10
4. Mme Vericel (300m) 17 rue Mesmorvan, Le Diben, 29630 Plougasnou 02 98 72 44 24 www.fournildepennarbed.com

Gite d'étape

5. Rando Plume Le Carnet de Bord (200m) 1 Route de Port Blanc, Le Diben, 29630 Plougasnou 02 24 69 33 54
6. Rando Plume de Kerdiès (500m) 5 Rue de Perhérel, St-Samson, 29630 Plougasnou 02 98 72 40 66 http://gite.kerdies.free.fr
   Open late February to December

Camping

7. Camping Bellevue (on route) 25, Route de la Corniche, Poul Rodou, 29241 Locquirec 02 98 78 80 80
8. Camping de la Baie de Térénez (on route) Moulin de Caneret, Térénez, 29252 Plouézoc'h 02 98 67 26 80 Open April to September www.campingbaiedeterenez.com

TRANSPORT

Train services: Morlaix station (02 98 15 20 05) on Paris/Brest main line. Branch line to Roscoff (30 mins) www.voyages-sncf.com

Bus services: timetable see www.tim-morlaix.com (02 98 88 82 82)

Lannion - Morlaix (via Locquirec)

Plougasnou - Morliax (via St-Jean-du-Doigt, Plougasnou, Primel Tregastel, Le Diben, St-Samson, Térénez, Dourduff-en-Mer)

Sucinio - Morlaix (ligne 2, route urbaine)

also Morlaix/Roscoff

Taxi: Guy Coant 02 98 67 34 54 Plougasnou
Guy Laviec 02 98 88 35 43 Morlaix

OTHER WALKS

It is possible to take a 9km circular walk around the promontory of Primel-Trégastel, returning by minor roads through Plougasnou.

The promontory of Barnenez provides a much shorter but equally rewarding circuit of about 4km.

GLOSSARY

aber - estuary

algue - seaweed

allée couverte - neolithic grave

anse - bay, creek

auberge - inn

auberge de jeunesse - youth hostel

baie - bay

balade - a walk

balisage - waymarking

bouchots - mussel beds

bourg - large village

calvaire - calvary

centre nautique -
  sailing/watersports centre

chambres d'hôte - B&B

chemin - small road, track, path

chemin creux - sunken track

commune - local administrative
  area/parish

Corps de Garde - guardhouse

corsair - licensed pirate

côte - coast

daymark - (see seamark)

dépot pain - point of sale for bread

digue - dike, bank

dolmen - neolithic/bronze age
  burial chamber

embarcadère - landing stage

enez - island

épicerie - grocery

étang - lake

fontaine - spring/fountain

four - oven

gîte d'étape - basic overnight
  accommodation

goémon - seaweed

grève - shore

halles - covered market

île - island

îlot - island, small island

La Poste - Post Office

lavoir - washing place

mairie - town hall

maison de retraite -
  old peoples' home

manoir - manor

menhir - standing stone

moules-frites - mussels with chips

moulin - mill

musée - museum

mytiliculture - musssel farming

naufrage - shipwreck

navette - shuttle service

ostreiculture - oyster farming

passerelle - footbridge

pays - local area, country

phare - lighthouse

plage - beach

port de plaisance - marina

presse (maison de la) - newsagent

quai - quay

rando-gîte/rando-plume -
  basic overnight
  accommodation specifically
  for walkers

relais - inn, staging post

rocher - rock

route - road

rue - street

seamark - navigation aid visible in
  daylight

sentier piéton - pedestrian
  footpath

sillon - spit of land/sandbank

vedette - passenger boat/ferry

vivier - fish tank

PLANNING

Whatever length of walk you are planning to undertake you will need to consider the maps you take with you, the clothing you wear or carry and the food and water you will need on the route.

Maps

Taking the maps first, those in this book, along with the accompanying text, should be quite sufficient to get you round without problems. Even so, to get a wider picture you might also like to take the appropriate 1:25,000 scale IGN map, the French equivalent of the British OS Explorer series. The numbers of those covering this route are: 1215OT Mont St-Michel to Cancale; 1116ET Cancale to St-Lunaire; 1016ET St-Lunaire to Sables d'Or-les-Pins; 0916ET Sables d'Or-les-Pins to Yffiniac; 0916OT Yffiniac to Plage Bonaparte; 0814OT Plage Bonaparte to the Anse de Gouermel; 0714OT the Anse de Gouermel to the Pointe de Séhar; and 0615ET Pointe de Séhar to Morlaix.

Clothing

Clothing needed will depend on the time of year you are planning to walk. July and August are probably best avoided if possible on account of the number of holiday makers, but almost all the rest of the year is suitable. Overall, Brittany can be expected to be just a little warmer than the UK. The bonus comes in winter, when the Gulf Stream raises Breton temperatures to levels rivalling those in the south of France. The downside is that, projecting so far to the west, the region can be wet when the rest of France has dry weather. But when the sun shines from a cloudless sky, there is, as anywhere, a real risk of sunburn (seriously – even in January!). So pack a waterproof, an extra sweater, a wide-brimmed hat, a long-sleeved shirt and some sun-cream and you will be able to cope with whatever it throws at you! Footwear likewise depends on the season. Boots would be the choice in winter, when even coastal tracks can be muddy and slippery. They also give the best support for rough cliff paths. But in summertime, a pair of good trainers will cope perfectly well, and be less heavy on your feet.

Provisions

The food you need depends on the length of time you will be out walking, but most importantly, make sure you carry enough water for the duration. Requirements are obviously increased in hot weather. On this coastal path you will pass many bars and restaurants, and stopping at one of these for lunch adds an extra dimension to the day. In towns, there is sure to be a restaurant open at any time of the year, but at some of the more remote beaches, restaurant opening is definitely seasonal – and even then they can always be closed at the whim of the proprietor. He may well be taking a day off, or even his own week's holiday, so it would be unwise to rely on any single restaurant for resuscitation. Always carry emergency rations!

Transport

Since walking along the coast is essentially linear walking, transport will be a necessary ingredient of your planning. Whether you are walking for a day, a week or a month, unless you have two cars, you will need to use public transport, or avail yourself of a local taxi. Relevant phone numbers and web sites are given with this in mind – and if you think language may be a problem in communication, the local Tourist Office should be able to help out. Day walkers may think it more relaxing to travel out by bus or taxi in the morning, returning at leisure to the place where the car waits to take them home.

Accommodation

The last element of planning is accommodation. In this holiday area there is more than enough and long-distance walkers should never have to walk too far between overnight stops. But it is worth noting that for the high season (July and August), all accommodation should be booked very early. This is also advisable if you are intending to end the day at an off-the-beaten-track spot where there may be only one chambre d'hôte or gîte d'étape available. Campsites will also need early booking in high season. Opening dates have been given (where they have been published) and it is worth checking them carefully before setting off.

Recommended Routes

Finally, and most importantly, where should you go? Below are just a few suggestions.

If you have a month –

Walk it all! The total distance from Mont St-Michel to Morlaix is 548 km, a very achievable average of about 18 km a day. Or if you are travelling from the UK, simplify things by taking the ferry crossing to St-Malo, walking to Morlaix, and then getting a quick bus ride (or even another walk) on to Roscoff for the crossing home. Brittany Ferries (www.brittany-ferries.com) can supply timetables and fares.

If you have a fortnight –

St-Brieuc is the natural break point and is connected by public transport to both St-Malo and Morlaix. The section to the east of St-Brieuc (227km) includes many renowned holiday resorts, while that to the west (321km) is generally more wild (although not entirely, because it includes the Pink Granite Coast)

If you have a week –

You can generally expect to walk around 20km a day, so the section between St-Malo and St-Brieuc (approx.150km) would not be impossible. Shorter but more energetic would be the interesting section between St-Brieuc and Tréguier (136km). Either could be cut short if you want to take things more easily.

If you have 3 or 4 days –

It has to be the Pink Granite Coast if you have never seen it before. The distance between Perros-Guirec and Lannion is 56km and there is a good bus service linking the towns.

Those who like their walking on the wilder side could go for the section between Locquirec and Morlaix – a mere 46km, but no easy amble over the cliff paths. Again the towns are connected by bus.

Only a day to spare?

Well, of course it will depend on where you are spending the rest of your holiday. But if this is determined by the walking, try

• Perros-Guirec to Trégastel (13km) for pure spectacle

• The circuit of Cap Fréhel (19km, but could be shortened) for grandeur

• Cancale to Rothéneuf (23km) for an unexpectedly beautiful stretch of coast close to St-Malo. To avoid transport complications, the 22km circuit of the Pointe du Grouin could be substituted

Journey Planner

Day	Destination	Accommodation	Contact

INDEX of PLACES

A listing of the main places mentioned, and better known headlands and beaches
(main reference is bolded)

Other Red Dog books
about Brittany

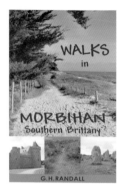

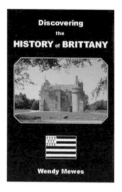

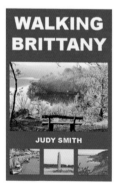

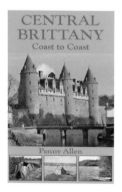

www.reddogbooks.com

BRITTANY WALKS ASSOCIATION

Brittany Walks is an association based in Finistere with the aim of promoting and developing walking and historical interest in Brittany through the medium of the English language.

The association organises events, including regular guided walks and outings, talks, courses and workshops in English. It also works with tourist organisations and other associations to help English speakers, of whatever nationality, to explore and discover the history and landscape of Brittany.

In addition, Brittany Walks provides an internet-based information service.

For details of the association, membership and events:

www.brittanywalks.com

WALKING THE
BRITTANY
COAST

VOL 2: MORLAIX TO BENODET
WENDY MEWES

www.reddogbooks.com